FABULOUSLY
FRENCH COOKING

Cathleen CLARITY

Kathrin KOSCHITZKI

FABULOUSLY FRENCH COOKING

70 Simple, Classic, and Chic Recipes for Every Occasion

Skyhorse Publishing

DEDICATION & THANKS

… to my sweet mom, Pat.

… to my sister, Ang, my angel.

… to my three musketeers: Cécilia, Bastien, and Bianca.

And very special thanks to the nice people at Callwey.

INTRODUCTION

My fascination with French cooking goes back many years to when I was a young girl growing up in Minnesota. At that time, fine cuisine was pretty much limited to a few fast food places and meatloaf. Thank goodness the food world has come a long way.

My favorite television program as a little girl was called *The French Chef* with Julia Child, the creator of the original "cooking show." Watching her prepare what seemed to be such complicated, involved recipes was absolutely mesmerizing to me. She would throw in a French word here and there and so sparked my curiosity. I knew I had to learn more. During my university studies, I spent three terms in Paris. The food, the style, and the beauty of the city were pure revelation! I couldn't wait to get back, and I moved to Paris immediately upon graduation. One of my favorite treats then, and still now, was a fresh, warm baguette early in the morning. It rarely made it back to my tiny apartment, however; I'd munch it all down on the walk back. You just can't get that satisfying taste anywhere else.

I haven't always been a chef. My professional life started in the public relations and communications field, but my underlying love of fantastic food had been dormant since childhood. After my third child was born, that desire became reality when I was accepted at École Ferrandi, a prestigious culinary school in Paris. What an incredible year that was! I was in the kitchen every day starting at 8 a.m., and my sole goal was to learn as much as possible; it was a dream come true. My new life as a professional chef started here.

After graduating from Ferrandi, I worked in a 2-star Michelin restaurant in Paris, which was enriching and exhausting! I quickly started my own catering company and became a private chef for several years. It was at this time that I developed my own style of cooking: market fresh, seasonal, light and bright with just a bit of cream and butter! The product itself is the star on the plate—no need to overwhelm with too many flavors at once. I like to keep my food clean and straightforward with the right dose of technique and a good sense of balance for seasoning and condiments.

My love of cooking naturally led itself to a love of teaching! I started my own cooking school and then had the pleasure of teaching for Chef Cyril Lignac in a beautiful Paris kitchen. I now give live online cooking lessons every evening for

L'atelier des Chefs. My favorite students are the timid ones. They appear a bit overwhelmed at first, but a few hours later, when the meal is prepared and they are enjoying it at the table, that look of pride on their faces is so satisfying.

The idea for writing this book came to me nearly two years ago. My students often asked me for menu ideas and ways to get organized in the kitchen, like a restaurant chef. I was happy to give them tips here and there, but they needed a bit more. There are so many great reasons to get together around a wonderful meal and coming up with the themes for the menus was a breeze.

Now all I needed was a great photographer with the same love of food as me. Kathrin, also a former Ferrandi student, was a gift from culinary heaven. The first time I saw the pictures on her blog, I literally got goosebumps. "She's the one!" I thought, and I contacted her immediately. Kathrin is a wonderful pastry chef and photographer. She has that whimsical eye for all that is sweet and is able to magically capture it in her images. We had a great time pulling the book together. I'd meticulously prepare my recipes in the fine French tradition, and when I had my head turned, Kathrin would poke her spoon into it before taking the picture, giving the dishes that human touch that so describes both of our styles.

I cooked and cooked, Kathrin shot and shot, and my kids ate and ate! We hope you will enjoy using our book as much as we enjoyed creating it for you.

M E N U   0 1

SPRING FAMILY LUNCH

Appetizers
Young Vegetables in Tempura
Green Asparagus with
Parmesan Shavings
Poached White Asparagus

Main Course
Slowly Roasted Veal Loin with
Chanterelles and Almonds

Dessert
Three-Berry Pavlova with Fresh
Whipped Cream

There's nothing better than the first signs of spring.

In France, the seasons are well defined in every way. The weather definitely tips you off, as does the general mood in the air. When spring has finally sprung, suddenly everything becomes light and airy and full of possibilities.

I love going to the markets in Paris at this time of year. After a long, often gray and rainy winter, the market stalls are finally brimming with all that is green, fresh, and leafy. The baby vegetables are vibrant and tasty, the young meats so tender, and the red fruit, dazzling and sweet. Letting the seasons guide you to the freshest ingredients in France is easy, but you'll be without good strawberries in February! You have to wait until nature says it's okay, and oh, is that wait worth it!

There is a wonderful tradition in France— *le déjeuner de dimanche*, or Sunday lunch. It's a time when you gather family together, all generations, and share a beautifully prepared meal, with wine, of course, that usually lasts well into the afternoon. My idea behind this lunch menu is to take the very best the spring market has to offer and turn it into something simple and fabulous. You'll find lots of professional tips to ease you through this menu and treat your family and friends to a wonderful weekend lunch in the garden!

APPETIZER

YOUNG VEGETABLES IN TEMPURA

Tempura Batter

3½ ounces (100 g)
all-purpose flour

1 teaspoon baking soda

2 tablespoons
cornstarch

1 egg

⅘ cup (20 cl) ice-cold
water

2 tablespoons poppy
seeds

Young Veggies

baby turnips with part
of their green tops

pink radishes with tips

french green beans

pencil carrots

mini beetroot

mini zucchini flowers

edible flowers: violets,
pansies

For Frying

½ gallon (2 L)
grapeseed oil

fleur de sel or Maldon
sea salt

TEMPURA. Sift together the flour, baking soda, and cornstarch. Whisk the egg with the cold water. Mix ⅓ of the flour mixture into the egg/water mixture using a fork. Repeat two more times until all of the flour mixture is blended. Do not overmix, or the gluten in the flour will develop and the batter will become heavy. The batter may have a few lumps, and this is fine.

Add the poppy seeds and mix lightly. For best results, use batter right after being made.

YOUNG VEGGIES. Wash all of the vegetables. Spring vegetables have a very thin skin and therefore don't need peeling, except for the beetroots.

FRYING. Heat the grapeseed oil in a heavy pan or deep fat fryer to 350°F (180°C).

Whisk the tempura batter and dip the vegetables into the batter in small quantities. Use a fork or chopsticks to take the veggies out of the batter, so that the excess batter will drip off.

Once the oil is to temperature, place the veggies delicately into the oil, about 4 to 5 at a time. Turn them around in the oil using a mesh skimmer.

Remove the vegetables once they are golden brown and place on paper towel to absorb excess oil.

Pile up on a serving platter, sprinkle with fleur de sel or Maldon sea salt, serve immediately. Believe me—these vegetables won't last long!

—

Serves 4. Prep time: 20 minutes. Cook time: 5 minutes.

APPETIZER

GREEN ASPARAGUS WITH PARMESAN SHAVINGS

18 local green asparagus shoots

sea salt

fruity olive oil

fresh ground pepper

¼ cup (50 g) parmesan cheese

Cut off the woody end of the asparagus. Green asparagus doesn't really need to be peeled, but I like to peel them lightly with a vegetable peeler; the contrast of the light green stems and dark green tips looks nice after peeling.

Boil a large quantity of water in a wide pan. The asparagus should lay flat. Once the water boils, add salt. The salt will help preserve the vivid green color.

Check the tenderness after 6 minutes by inserting the tip of a knife into one of the stems. The asparagus should be slightly firm.

Strain the asparagus and place immediately into a large quantity of ice-cold water. This will fix the chlorophyll, keeping the asparagus appetizingly green.

Place the asparagus onto a large platter, and just before serving, sprinkle with some good olive oil, season with freshly ground pepper; shave fresh parmesan over the top using a vegetable peeler.

—

Along with white asparagus (page 19), 6 servings.
Prep time: 40 minutes. Cook time: 20 minutes.

APPETIZER

POACHED WHITE ASPARAGUS

from the Landes region of France in Herbed Sauce Mousseline

---

18 white asparagus

Sauce Mousseline

1 egg at room
temperature

1 teaspoon French
mustard

8½ fl. ounces (25 cl)
grapeseed oil

fleur de sel

¼ bunch flat parsley

¼ bunch cilantro

¼ bunch chives

¼ bunch tarragon

juice of ½ lemon

black pepper

chives, for garnishing

ASPARAGUS. Peel the asparagus with a vegetable peeler. Sometimes white asparagus can be pretty woody. Cut off the fibrous end so that all of the asparagus are the same size. Boil a large quantity of water in a wide pan. The asparagus should lay flat. Once the water boils, add sea salt.

Check the tenderness after approximately 12 minutes; the white asparagus should be cooked to more tender than the green. Plunge the asparagus into ice-cold water to stop the cooking process.

Strain off water and place the asparagus onto a plate covered with paper towels to absorb excess water. Let chill in the refrigerator.

SAUCE MOUSSELINE. Prepare a classic mayonnaise: all of the ingredients must be at room temperature. Separate the yolk and egg white. Keep the egg white in a clean bowl. Whisk the yolk with the mustard, pour the grapeseed oil slowly while whisking briskly. The mayonnaise should take quickly, becoming quite creamy. Add the lemon juice, season with fleur de sel, and fresh ground pepper.

Whisk the egg white until it becomes frothy and creamy, but not too stiff. Wash all of the herbs and chop finely. Add the frothy egg white to the mayonnaise delicately using a spatula. Add all of the chopped herbs. Check the seasoning.

Serve the asparagus on a large platter with the *sauce mousseline* on top. Garnish with chives.

—

Along with green asparagus (page 16) 6 servings.
Prep time: 40 minutes. Cook time: 20 minutes.

MAIN COURSE

SLOWLY ROASTED VEAL LOIN

with Chanterelles and Almonds

Veal Loin

1 (approximately 3 pounds [1.5 kg]) veal loin.*

2 sweet white onions

½ bunch of fresh sage

6 tablespoons olive oil

butter (optional)

⅔ cup (15 cl) dry white wine

1 quart (1 l) veal stock

salt and pepper

—

*Have your butcher tie the loin up like a roast. (Ask your butcher for some veal bones.)

VEAL LOIN. Preheat oven to 360°F (180°C). Take the meat out of the refrigerator at least 1 hour before cooking. Peel and slice the onions, and wash and spin dry the fresh sage.

Heat a cast-iron Dutch oven with 3 tablespoons of olive oil and sweat the onions along with the fresh sage leaves. The onions should not brown. Remove the onions and keep aside in a bowl.

Season the veal on all sides with fine salt. Heat 3 more tablespoons of oil in the Dutch oven and brown the loin on all sides. Add the veal bones; they should brown, as well. You can add a little fresh butter to help the browning. Spoon the melted butter over the loin roast regularly. The meat should be well browned, almost caramelized but not burned.

Remove the browned meat from the Dutch oven, remove excess fat, heat the meat juices in the Dutch oven, and deglaze with the dry white wine. Let the alcohol evaporate.

Put the veal loin back into the Dutch oven, add the onions and fresh sage leaves, cover in veal stock, and bring to a boil. Cover with lid and place in oven for 1 hour. Turn the roast over after 30 minutes of cooking.

After 1 hour, remove the roast from the Dutch oven, place on a rack over a pan and cover with foil. The roast must rest at least 15 minutes before being sliced.

Place the Dutch oven on the stove and reduce the cooking juices. Strain the juices into a small saucepan and heat. If desired, add a tablespoon of sweet butter and whisk briskly to thicken the sauce and make it velvety.

Slice the roast and place on a serving platter and pour some sauce over the top. Serve the rest of the sauce in a sauce dish.

MENU 01 – SPRING FAMILY LUNCH

Chanterelles with Almonds and Lemon

1.75 pounds (800 g) chanterelles

3 spring onions

3 tablespoons olive oil

fleur de sel

10 g of sweet butter

1 preserved lemon (preserved in salt)

lemon zest

12 fresh peeled almonds

fresh ground pepper

CHANTERELLES. Cut off the end of the stem. Slice the larger mushrooms in two, and wash all of the mushrooms rapidly in a large bowl of water. Remove them quickly from the water and spin them dry in a salad spinner. Wash the spring onions and slice them at an angle.

Heat 3 tablespoons of olive oil in a heavy frying pan. Cook the mushrooms on high heat, salt and cook for 1 minute, until they render their natural liquid.

Strain off the liquid, remove the mushrooms. Add the sweet butter, and when the butter becomes frothy, add the mushrooms and the spring onions; cook for a few more minutes to brown the mushrooms.

Rinse the preserved lemon and slice in a fine julienne. Zest the lemon using a microplane. Add the lemon julienne and the zest, then the almonds. Heat gently.

Serve the warm mushrooms with the veal loin.

—

Veal: 6 servings. Prep time: 30 minutes. Cook time: 1 hour.
Chanterelles: 6 servings. Prep time: 20 minutes. Cook time: 10 minutes.

FABULOUSLY FRENCH COOKING – 21

DESSERT

THREE-BERRY PAVLOVA

with Fresh Whipped Cream

Meringue

6¾ fl. ounce (200 g) egg white

7 ounces (200 g) granulated sugar

7 ounces (200 g) powdered sugar

Fresh Whipped Cream

about 1¼ fl. ounces (33 cl) of full fat whipping cream

strawberries

raspberries

blueberries

Tips from a Pro

The best way to bake meringue for the pavlova is in an conventional electric oven at low heat. If using a gas oven, place the baking sheets as far away as possible from the heat source, usually at the bottom of the oven. This will prevent the meringue from burning the on bottom.

Preheat oven to 190°F (90°C). Prepare the meringue. Weigh all of the ingredients before starting.

MERINGUE. Whip the egg whites with an electric mixer. When the egg whites become frothy, start adding the granulated sugar, little by little. This will stiffen them and make them shiny. When the egg whites are stiff, stop whipping and add the powder sugar. Mix gently with a spatula.

Cover a baking sheet with parchment paper. Spread the meringue evenly, creating a thick disc shape. Scoop out the center; this is where the whipped cream and fresh berries will be placed once the meringue is baked and cooled.

Place a second baking sheet under the first one. This will prevent the meringue from burning on the bottom. Place the oven rack in the middle and bake the meringue for 70 minutes.

The meringue should be very white. Once baked, remove from oven and slide the parchment paper onto a rack to cool thoroughly.

WHIPPED CREAM. Place the whipping cream in the refrigerator for at least 30 minutes. Then, whip the cream slowly at first and then more and more rapidly until the cream thickens and becomes firm. This will take about 8 minutes.

ASSEMBLE THE PAVLOVA. Place the meringue on a serving platter. Fill the scooped out section with whipped cream. Add the fresh washed berries in the center and sprinkle with powdered sugar.

The pavlova may be held in the refrigerator up to an hour but should be eaten the same day.

———

6 servings. Prep time: 25 minutes. Cook time: 70 minutes.

MENU 02

LADIES' LUNCH

Appetizers
Grilled and Raw Salmon Bites in Citrus
Vinaigrette with Borage Flowers
Soft-Boiled Organic Eggs and Oven-Roasted
Beets with Goat Cheese Emulsion

Main Course
Free-Range Chicken Breast Rolls Stuffed with
Fresh Seasonal Herbs with French Green Beans,
Sweet Peas, and White Beans in Pistachio Pesto

Dessert
Cardamom Custard and Caramel-Covered
Green Grapes

What would I do without my best friends? They have followed me throughout my crazy culinary adventures, given advice, and tasted just about everything. They helped me get through the bad times and are there to celebrate the good. We have all been friends for years, our children are friends, and I think even our dogs like to hang out together! For this special lunch, I wanted to truly delight the ladies with the fresh, seasonal, light and tasty menu they deserve. It's the kind of meal where you feel as good afterwards as you did while eating it.

The cooking methods used are simple: poaching, boiling in water, and baking in a water bath. However, the sauces, condiments, and emulsions are slightly more elaborate. They add a luscious, satisfying finish to the dishes.

From appetizer to dessert, the conversation flowed and flowed, as did the rosé, and at the end of the meal, when it was time to go home, we all promised to do lunch much more often. Then the inevitable question came up—"Whose turn is it next?"—to which I invariably answered, "Don't worry, ladies, I'll do the cooking."

APPETIZER

GRILLED AND RAW SALMON BITES

in Citrus Vinaigrette with Borage Flowers

Melba toasts

1¾ fl. ounce (50 g) clarified butter

4 slices of good white bread or "pain de mie"

Salmon

1 pound (500 g) wild salmon filet

zest and juice of 2 lemons

zest and juice of 2 limes

1 tablespoon soy sauce

3 teaspoons sesame seed oil

3 tablespoons olive oil

sea salt, pepper

borage flowers

MELBA TOASTS. Make the clarified butter by melting about 5 ounces (150 g) of butter over a water bath. Fully melt and continue heating until the butter separates and the solids fall to the bottom, leaving only the butter fat on the top. Filter through a cheesecloth to remove any traces of foam.

Brush the bread with the clarified butter on both sides and place on a baking sheet covered in parchment paper. Cover with parchment paper, place a second baking sheet over the top, and bake at 350°F (180°C) for approximately 20 minutes. The bread will become golden brown on both sides without having to turn it over. Using clarified butter will keep the butter from over-browning or burning. When cool, cut the bread into 1½ inch squares.

SALMON. Slice the salmon into 1-inch cubes. You will need a total of 24 cubes. Whisk together the juice of one lime and one lemon, soy sauce, and 3 teaspoons of sesame seed oil. Marinate 12 of the salmon cubes, cover with plastic wrap, and keep refrigerated. For the other 12 cubes, season with fine salt and pepper, heat 1 tablespoon of olive oil in a frying pan, and sear the salmon cubes on both sides, approximately 3 minutes per side. Remove to absorbent paper. Whisk the remaining citrus juices together with salt, pepper, and olive oil. Add the zests.

TO SERVE. Start with a golden brown melba toast, add one cube of grilled salmon, then a cube of marinated salmon. Top with a few drops of vinaigrette and finish with a borage flower, which tastes amazingly like oysters.

———

Serves 4. Prep time: 15 minutes. Cooking time: 24 minutes.

APPETIZER

SOFT-BOILED ORGANIC EGGS AND OVEN-ROASTED BEETS

with Goat Cheese Emulsion

Beets

2 yellow beets

1 orange beet

1 red beet

pinch of sugar

pinch of salt

olive oil

Eggs

4 organic eggs

Goat Cheese Emulsion

6¾ fl. ounces (200 g) whipping cream

about ½ cup (100 g) goat cheese

1⅔ cups (50 g) whole milk, cold

30 toasted hazelnuts

beet leaves, for garnish

salt, pepper

BEETS. Rinse and dry all but one yellow beet and place them on a large piece of parchment paper. Sprinkle with a pinch of sugar, a pinch of salt, and drizzle with olive oil. Fold the parchment paper at the top and on the sides, then fold under, making a tightly closed pouch. Place on a baking sheet and roast in a 350°F (180°) oven for 1 hour. Oven-roasting the beets will develop their natural sugars and make them melt-in-the-mouth delicious.

Thinly slice the remaining yellow beet using a mandoline. Cut the slices into prefect circles using a small round cookie cutter. Keep the beet rounds crisp by placing them in ice-cold water until ready to use.

SOFT-BOILED EGGS. Boil a large pot of water, plunge the eggs carefully into the boiling water, and set a timer for 5 minutes. Prepare a bowl of ice-cold water and plunge the cooked eggs in the cold water to stop the cooking. Once the eggs are thoroughly cooled, peel them in the cold water; this makes it easier to keep the eggs perfectly round without damaging the white. Set the eggs aside on absorbent paper.

GOAT CHEESE EMULSION. Melt the goat cheese into the cream in a medium saucepan on medium heat. Season with black pepper. Set aside. When the beets are fully cooked, remove from oven and let cool. Peel them using a paring knife and slice into quarters.

Reheat the eggs by plunging them into a pot of simmering water for 30 seconds.

TO SERVE. Dress the appetizer in a soup plate: arrange a quarter of each beet, place the warm egg over the top, and cut open halfway. The yolk should be honey-colored and slowly pour out onto the beets. Heat the goat cheese emulsion to just boiling. Mix using a hand blender. Add the cold milk and mix the surface of the cream to create foam. The cold milk added to the hot emulsion will make the foam firmer.

Cover the egg with the frothy emulsion. Add the raw beets and the beet leaves, and sprinkle with toasted hazelnuts and sea salt.

—

Serves 4. Prep time: 30 minutes. Cooking time: 1 hour 10 minutes.

MAIN COURSE

FREE-RANGE CHICKEN BREAST ROLLS STUFFED WITH FRESH SEASONAL HERBS

with French Green Beans, Sweet Peas, and White Beans in Pistachio Pesto

---

Chicken Jus

1 pound (500 g) chicken wings

olive oil

salted butter

⅔ cup (15 cl) dry white wine

½ carrot, diced

1 white onion, diced

1 quart (1 l) veal stock, room temperature

Green Vegetables

1 pound (500 g) French green beans

2.25 pounds (1 kg) sweet peas

2.25 (1 kg) fresh white beans (cannellini, borlotti)

2 tablespoons olive oil

½ quart (½ l) chicken stock

—

Tips from a Pro

When preparing the jus, remove the skin from the chicken wings before browning. This will make the jus richer in taste and less greasy overall.

CHICKEN JUS. Brown the chicken wings in olive oil in a medium saucepan, add 1 tablespoon of salted butter and continue browning. Deglaze with the white wine, and scrape the bottom of the saucepan using a spatula to detach the caramelized brown bits. Let the alcohol evaporate, approximately 2 minutes. Add the diced carrot and onion. Add a bit more butter if necessary to brown the vegetables. Strain the meat and vegetables to remove excess fat. Put all back into the saucepan and add the veal stock. Bring to a boil then reduce heat and simmer for 40 minutes. Skim if necessary.

Strain through a fine sieve into a small saucepan and reduce to half. The jus will thicken slightly and should cover the spoon. Keep warm.

GREEN VEGETABLES. Remove the ends of the green beans, and shell the peas and beans. Boil a large pot of salted water. Plunge the green beans and peas into the water. Cook for approximately 5 to 6 minutes and then plunge into ice-cold water to stop the cooking and preserve the vibrant green color. Once cooled, remove to absorbent paper.

Heat 2 tablespoons of olive oil in a frying pan and add the fresh white beans. Coat in olive oil and heat through. Add the chicken stock and simmer for 20 minutes until the beans are tender.

Slice the cooled green beans into quarter-inch pieces. Add the peas and green beans into the pan with the white beans. Add a bit of salted butter, about a ½ cup of chicken stock, and heat through. The butter and chicken stock will thicken a bit and make a glaze giving the vegetables a nice sheen. Season with salt and pepper and keep warm.

Chicken

4 free-range chicken
breasts

½ bunch fresh
cilantro, Thai basil,
chives, chive flowers

salt, pepper

Pesto

about ¼ cup (50 g)
pistachios

about 1 cup (200 g)
rocket arugula

1 clove garlic

about ¼ cup (50 g)
parmesan

6¾ fl. ounces (200 ml)
olive oil

sea salt

chives flowers, for
garnishing

CHICKEN. Flatten the chicken breasts and remove any excess fat using a paring knife. Wash, dry, and mince the fresh herbs. Lay out a rectangular piece of heat-resistant plastic wrap, two times longer than the chicken breast. Place the flattened chicken breast in the center of the plastic wrap toward the bottom. Season with salt and pepper; add the mixed fresh herbs by spreading them across the chicken breast in a straight line. Roll the chicken breast tightly in the plastic wrap. Take the ends of the wrap and continue rolling breast into a log shape. Tie the ends of the wrap tightly.

Boil a large pot of water, add the chicken rolls, cover the pot, and remove from heat. Poach for 20 minutes. Remove from pot and let cool slightly. Remove the plastic wrap and slice in half-inch slices. Keep warm.

ROCKET AND PISTACHIO PESTO. Toast pistachios in a small frying pan with no added fat. Wash and spin-dry the rocket salad. Peel the garlic and remove the green germ. Grate the fresh parmesan. Add all ingredients to the food processor bowl and process to a paste texture. Add the olive oil in a steady small stream while food processor is running until all oil has been incorporated. Remove to a small serving bowl.

FOR SERVING

Place a good amount of warm vegetables in the center of the plate. Top with 3 slices of the chicken roll, sprinkle with a little sea salt, and finish with chive flowers. Serve the chicken jus and the pesto on the side.

—

Serves 4. Prep time: 50 minutes. Cook time: 1 hour 30 minutes.

DESSERT

CARDAMOM CUSTARD

and Caramel-Covered Green Grapes

Custard

1 vanilla bean

1 pint (50 cl) whole milk

1 teaspoon ground cardamom

6 egg yolks

3½ ounces (100 g) sugar

Caramel Grapes

8.8 ounces (250 g) sugar

½ cup (100 g) water

juice of ½ lemon

30 green grapes

For this recipe, only the yolks are required. The eggs can be stored in a clean, airtight container for up to three days in a refrigerator and used to make meringues or macarons.

CUSTARD. Slice the vanilla pod in two and scrape out the seeds using the tip of a knife. Heat the milk with the vanilla to boil. Add the cardamom, remove from heat, and infuse for 20 minutes. Whisk the egg yolks and the sugar in a medium-sized mixing bowl, pour the warm milk over the eggs, and strain through a fine sieve.

Preheat oven to 340°F (170°). Position 6 small cups or ramekins in a large baking dish. Fill with the milk/egg mixture. Place baking dish in oven and fill with boiling water to half the height of the cups. Cover with foil and bake for 40 minutes. Remove from oven and let cool. Place in refrigerator until ready to serve. The custard may be prepared up to 2 days in advance and kept in the refrigerator.

CARAMEL GRAPES. Mix the sugar, water, and lemon juice in a medium saucepan. Bring to a boil then continue heating to 300°F (150°C). Dip the grapes into the caramel using tweezers. Place the caramel-covered grapes onto a nonstick baking mat and let cool.

Serve the custard chilled with the caramel grapes.

———

Serves 6. Prep time: 40 minutes. Cook time: 48 minutes.

MENU 03

LUNCH FOR TEENS

Main Course
Free-Range Chicken Keftas with Homemade Tartar Sauce and Toasted Pita Bread

Side Dishes
Thick-Cut Sweet Potato Fries Tossed in
Turmeric

Caesar Salad with Crunchy Garlic Croutons

Organic Carrot Salad with Toasted
Hazelnuts, Orange Sections, and Hazelnut
Vinaigrette

Dessert
Mango Litchi Smoothie

Jumbo-Sized Chocolate Butter Cookies

My advice for kids and food is to get them into the kitchen as young as possible and show them how to make a few simple dishes. Home-made food just always tastes better than fast food and takeaway, and they will be so proud and want to invite their friends over to enjoy the great food they've prepared themselves.

You're killing two birds with one stone here by teaching the importance of eating well and also how to be gracious hosts and hostesses.

The recipes in this chapter can fit into just about any season, but they seem to work particularly well in early autumn as a pre-back-to-school lunch gathering. The food here is so tasty without the fuss or the dishes, and the menu has a great street food feeling, with a healthy twist. I'm sure your kids will love it— mine certainly did!

MAIN COURSE

FREE-RANGE CHICKEN KEFTAS

with Homemade Tartar Sauce and Toasted Pita Bread

Chicken

3 free-range chicken breasts

2 spring onions

2 cloves garlic

fresh cilantro (the leaves of 8 sprigs)

fresh mint (the leaves of 4 sprigs)

1 tablespoon ground turmeric

1 tablespoon Moroccan spices (Ras el Hanout)

3 tablespoons olive oil

salt, pepper

1 lemon

2 vine ripe tomatoes

4 leaves iceberg lettuce

8 pita breads

Tangy Tartar Sauce

(makes approximately 10.5 ounces/300 g)

1 organic egg yolk

1 tablespoon or sweet mustard

6¾ fl. ounces (20 cl) grapeseed oil

juice of ½ lemon

salt, pepper

½ white onion, finely chopped

10 sprigs Italian parsley, chopped

small handful capers

10 baby pickles, chopped

CHICKEN. Grind the chicken breasts in the food processor. Remove to a bowl and season with salt and pepper.

Finely chop the spring onions, including the green tops. Peel the garlic, remove the germ, and chop finely. Wash, dry, and finely chop the fresh herbs.

Mix the turmeric and Moroccan spices and then sprinkle over the chicken. Add olive oil and mix well. Roll into 1-inch balls, and flatten them to make patties.

Heat olive oil in a heavy skillet or on a grill pan and brown the keftas on both sides, approximately 6 minutes in total. Remove to absorbent paper.

Thinly slice the tomatoes and finely chop the lettuce. Warm the pita bread in a 350°F (180°C) oven for 5 minutes.

Build your sandwich with three kefta patties, lettuce, tomatoes, and lots of tartar sauce.

TANGY TARTAR SAUCE. Make sure all ingredients are room temperature before starting. Place the egg yolk in a dry bowl. Whisk in the mustard and then whisk in the oil, little by little. The mayonnaise should be light in color and very creamy. Add the lemon juice and season with salt and pepper. Add the chopped onion, parsley, capers, and pickles. Check seasoning. Cover and keep chilled until ready for use.

—

Serves 4. Prep time: 30 minutes. Cook time: 6 minutes.

SIDE DISH

THICK-CUT SWEET POTATO FRIES TOSSED IN TURMERIC

3 medium-sized sweet potatoes

4 tablespoons olive oil

2 tablespoons turmeric

sea salt

black pepper

Preheat oven to 300°F (150°C).

Peel the sweet potatoes. Cut them in $\frac{1}{2}$-inch-thick slices, turn, and slice in $\frac{1}{2}$-inch-thick sticks. Place the sticks in a large mixing bowl. Add the olive oil, turmeric, sea salt, and pepper and toss thoroughly. The sweet potatoes should be coated with oil and spices. You can prepare this step in advance because sweet potatoes, unlike white potatoes, will not oxidize with air contact.

Place a single layer on a baking sheet covered with parchment paper. Bake for approximately 15 to 20 minutes. The fries should be slightly crispy but moist inside.

Serve in small french fry boxes if available.

—

Serves 4. Prep time: 15 minutes. Cook time: 15 to 20 minutes.

SIDE DISH

CAESAR SALAD

with Crunchy Garlic Croutons

Croutons

5 thick slices sour-
dough bread

olive oil

2 cloves garlic

sea salt, black pepper

Salad

1 head fresh romaine
lettuce

fresh parmesan

Caesar Dressing

1 hard-boiled egg

1 egg yolk

1 clove garlic

4 anchovies, rinsed

about ¼ cup (50 g)
parmesan, grated

8½ fl. ounces (25 cl)
olive oil

juice of 1 lemon

1 teaspoon red wine
vinegar

Tabasco

Worcestershire sauce

pepper

CROUTONS. Cut the sourdough bread into cubes. Heat the olive oil in a heavy skillet; peel and add the garlic cloves. Toast the croutons in the oil until golden. Remove to absorbent paper and season with sea salt and black pepper.

SALAD. Wash the lettuce, spin dry, and slice the leaves in 2 or 3 pieces depending on the size. Set aside.

CAESAR DRESSING. Roughly chop the hard-boiled egg and place in the bowl of a food processor. Add the egg yolk, the garlic clove (degermed), the rinsed anchovies, and grated parmesan. Mix. Add oil little by little, as the sauce becomes thick and creamy. Add the lemon juice, the vinegar, Tabasco, and Worcestershire sauce to taste.

SERVE. Toss the lettuce with the dressing. Lettuce should be lightly coated.

Serve in small salad bowls with croutons and shaved parmesan. Season with freshly ground black pepper.

—

Serves 12. Prep time: 30 minutes.

SIDE DISH

ORGANIC CARROT SALAD

with Toasted Hazelnuts, Orange Sections, and Hazelnut Vinaigrette

Salad

4 fresh organic carrots

1¾ cups (50 g) hazelnuts, peeled

2 juicy oranges

Vinaigrette

1 juice orange

1 tablespoon white balsamic vinegar

1 teaspoon honey

salt, pepper

2 tablespoon olive oil

2 tablespoons hazelnut oil

SALAD. Peel the carrots and grate finely. Place into a mixing bowl. Toast the hazelnuts in a hot frying pan without any oil. Turn the pan regularly to toast the hazelnuts on all sides. When toasted, (about 4 minutes) transfer to a cutting board and chop into small pieces using a chef's knife.

Peel two of the oranges using a paring knife to be sure to remove the pith. Remove the wedges by cutting on either side of the white sections. Slice the wedges in 3 equal pieces and add to the carrots. Add the chopped hazelnuts, mix together.

VINAIGRETTE. Press the juice of one orange. Add the white balsamic vinegar, whisk in the honey, sea salt, and pepper. Whisk in the two oils to make an emulsion. Check seasoning.

Season the salad and toss thoroughly. Serve in individual salad bowls.

——

Serves 4. Prep time: 20 minutes.

DESSERT

MANGO LITCHI SMOOTHIE

1 ripe mango

13½ fl. ounces (400 ml can) of litchis in light syrup

2 plain yogurts

6¾ fl. ounces (20 cl) fresh milk

ice cubes

fresh mint, if desired

Peel the mango, cut into thick slices. Drain the litchis, save the juice. Place fruit into blender, add the yogurt and milk. Add 5 ice cubes. Blend at high speed for several minutes. If a bit thick, add some litchi juice.

Poor into chilled glasses and place in fridge until ready to serve. Garnish with mint, if desired.

—

Serves 4. Prep time: 10 minutes.

DESSERT

JUMBO-SIZED CHOCOLATE BUTTER COOKIES

about 6 fl. ounces (180 g) good quality sweet butter

3¼ ounces (90 g) sugar

8¾ ounces (250 g) flour

1 pinch cinnamon

½ ounce (15 g) cocoa powder

These butter cookies do not have any egg. When baked, they become deliciously crispy!

Preheat oven to 350°F (180°C).

Cream the butter and sugar at medium speed in a mixer. Add the flour, cinnamon, and cocoa powder. Mix well.

Separate the dough into three parts. Roll each section into a large sausage shape. Cover in plastic wrap and let chill in the refrigerator for 20 minutes. When thoroughly chilled, remove wrap and slice round cookies ½-inch thick.

Place on a baking sheet covered with parchment paper and bake for 15 to 20 minutes. Let cool on rack. Serve with the smoothie.

—

Serves 8. Prep time: 15 minutes. Cook time: 15 to 20 minutes.

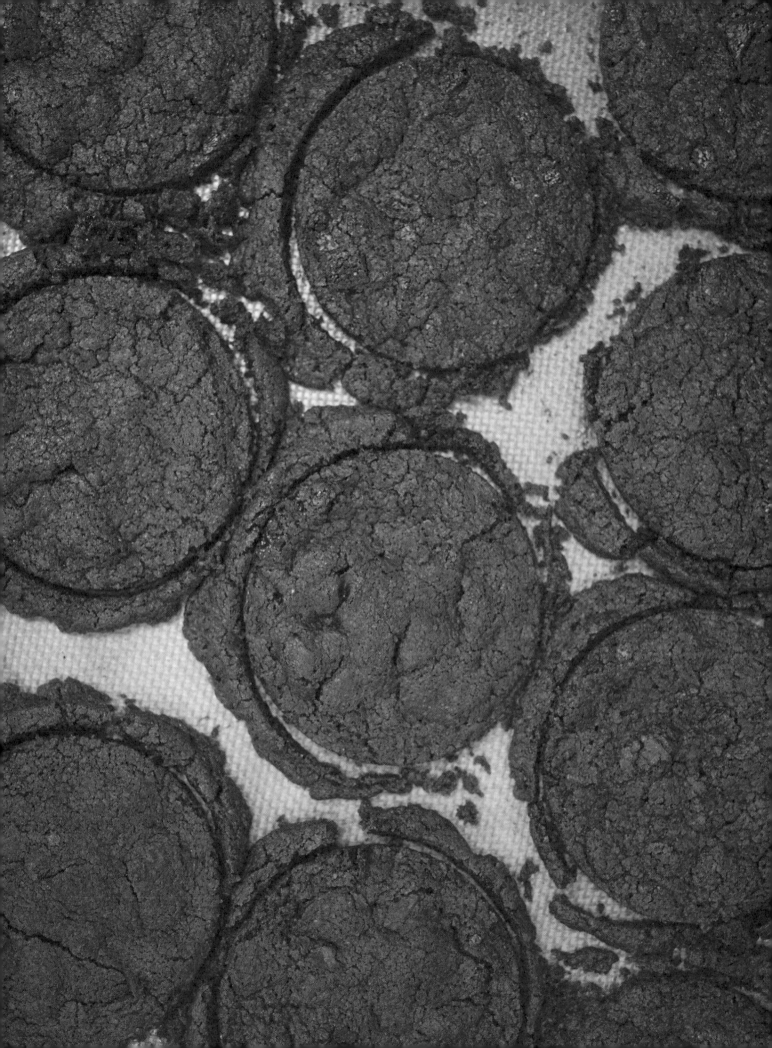

MENU 04

SATURDAY NIGHT DINNERS—
BACK FROM THE FISH MARKET

Appetizers

Sea Bream Tartare with Spring Onions, Wakame,
and Grilled Sesame Seeds

Fresh Mussels *Marinière* with a Handful of Fresh
Herbs

Prawn Ravioli with Baby Fava Beans in a Light
Prawn Broth

Main Course

Filet of Brill *à la Dugléré*

Dessert

Fresh Seasonal Fruit Poached in a Verbena Syrup
with Salty Butter Cookies and Sweet Wine
Sabayon

I love Saturday night dinners! Since living in France, I've really learned the importance of this particular evening.

Weeknights are reserved for business entertaining, simple family dinners, or restaurant dining, but Saturday nights are different and special. It's the night you invite others into your home.

The meal is always well-planned; invitations are made sometimes weeks in advance, and you can expect your guests to dress for dinner.

The outdoor markets are often on Saturdays in France so it is easy to find the freshest ingredients for your menu. Morning is filled up with the shopping and, after a light lunch, they use the afternoon to do all of the prep work. This will assure that your dinner will be a breeze.

The next three chapters will give you a large selection of menu ideas and tips for successfully hosting your own Saturday dinners. I've also added hints that will help you be at the table with your guests and not always in the kitchen.

Go ahead and set a beautiful table, light lots of candles, and just simply enjoy!

APPETIZER

SEA BREAM TARTARE

with Spring Onions, Wakame, and Grilled Sesame Seeds

---

4 sea bream filets without the skin

2 spring onions with the green tips

zest and juice of 2 organic lemons

grilled sesame seeds

dried wakame seaweed

fleur de sel

3 tablespoons sesame oil

May be made in advance and chilled, but season just before serving.

Prepare the sea bream filets by removing the stomach portion and all dark traces. Cut into small cubes. Wash the spring onions and dice them finely. Zest the lemons, using a microplane, and squeeze the juice.

In a small bowl, mix the cubes of sea bream, onions, lemon zest, and juice, and add the sesame seeds. Season with dried wakame seaweed, fleur de sel, and sesame oil.

Keep chilled until ready to serve. Use a small rectangular mold to plate the appetizer.

—

Serves 6. Prep time: 25 minutes.

APPETIZER

FRESH MUSSELS *MARINIÈRE*

with a Handful of Fresh Herbs

6½ pounds (3 kg) fresh mussels

2 large sweet white onions

about ¼ cup (50 g) salted butter

olive oil

mix of fresh herbs, as desired, such as dill, cilantro, parsley, or chives

2 cups (50 cl) dry white wine

fresh ground black pepper

Clean the mussels. If they're slightly opened, tap on the shell with your fingernail. If they close up again, the mussel is alive, hence very fresh. Peel and dice the onions. Wash all of the herbs and finely chop the leaves. Save the nicer stems, such as dill flowers.

Place the butter in a large pot, heat to frothy. Add the onions and the herb stems. Add the white wine, let it reduce a bit, as the alcohol needs to evaporate. Pour in the cleaned mussels. Slightly increase the heat and cover the pan. The mussels will open from the steam. Stir to mix the mussels and onions.

When the mussels are open, about 5 to 8 minutes, add the fresh cut herbs and mix gently. Season with fresh ground pepper but no salt—mussels are salty enough. Serve the mussels hot in a small bowl per person with a ladle of the juice on top. Finish with dill flowers.

—

Serves 6. Prep time: 15 minutes. Cook time: 8 minutes.

APPETIZER

PRAWN RAVIOLI

with Baby Fava Beans in a Light Prawn Broth

Ravioli

1 small bunch fresh parsley (or chervil)

3 spring onions

12 fresh prawns

2 tablespoons olive oil

Salt, pepper

½ cup (10 cl) dry white wine

about ¾ cup (200 g) fresh fava beans

about 1⅔ fl. ounces (5 cl) fresh cream

1 package Chinese wonton wrappers

1 egg white

rice flour

The ravioli may be made a few hours in advance and kept refrigerated.

Wash and chop the parsley and finely dice the spring onions. Peel the prawns, but keep the heads and shells. Make an incision on the back of the prawns and remove the intestine with the tip of your knife. Heat the olive oil in a heavy frying pan. Cook the prawns over high heat quickly, about 3 minutes. Remove to absorbent paper. Season with salt and pepper. Deglaze with the white wine. Let the alcohol evaporate; reduce the liquid a bit.

Blanch the fava beans in boiling salted water, strain, and plunge into ice-cold water to fix the chlorophyll. Strain again and place on absorbent paper to remove excess water.

Mix the sliced prawns, fava beans, spring onions, and parsley plus a little fresh cream in a small bowl. Season with salt and pepper.

Place a heaping teaspoon of prawn filling in the middle of the wonton wrapper. Paint the edges with egg white (the glue). Join the two diagonal angles, seal, then the two other diagonal angles, and seal well using your fingertips. The ravioli should look like a small pouch. Place the finished ravioli on a plate, sprinkle with rice flour, and keep in the refrigerator until ready to cook.

Boil a large quantity of water with sea salt. Drop the ravioli in three by three. When they come up to the surface, count about 45 seconds and they'll be done. Remove quickly with a slotted spoon.

Prawn Broth

1 white onion

parsley stems and fresh cilantro

2 tablespoons olive oil

heads and shells of the prawns used for the ravioli

1 cup (25 cl) dry white wine

1 quart (1 l) of shellfish stock (good brand, like Ariake)

1 white onion

high-quality soy sauce

——

Tips from a Pro

French cooking is all about taste and needs to be developed layer by layer. For this menu, make the prawn broth in advance and let it simmer gently. Warming it up the next day will give it an even richer flavor.

Broth may be made three days in advance and kept in the refrigerator. It may also be frozen until ready for use.

PRAWN BROTH. Dice the onions and wash the cilantro and parsley. Heat the olive oil in large pan. Brown the heads and shells of the prawns over high heat. Crush them down a bit to get as much flavor as possible. Add the diced onions and let sweat a few minutes. Deglaze with the white wine, heat to evaporate alcohol.

Pour in the shellfish stock, add the cooking juices from the prawns, bring to boil, then reduce heat and let simmer for 30 minutes. Filter into a clean pan and keep warm. Add a few drops of good soy sauce, check the seasoning. Add fresh cilantro leaves.

SERVE. Place three ravioli per person in a warm soup bowl and pour piping hot prawn broth on top.

——

Ravioli—Serves 6. Prep time: 30 minutes. Cook time: 23 minutes.

Broth—Serves 6. Prep time: 15 minutes. Cook time: 30 minutes.

MAIN COURSE

FILET OF BRILL *À LA DUGLÉRÉ*

4 brill filets with skin (about 5 ounces or 150 g/filet)

2 shallots

½ bunch flat parsley

3 fresh vine ripe tomatoes

2 cups (50 cl) fish stock, room temperature

about ⅔ fl. ounces (20 g) salted butter

The sauce base and fish may be prepared in advance. Cooking the brill is quick and must be done just before serving.

Remove the skin and stomach section of the brill filets and give them a nice shape. Finely dice the shallots and the flat parsley.

Peel the tomatoes with a tomato peeler, or by plunging them into boiling water 30 seconds, then into ice-cold water. The skin is then easily removed. Cut into quarters, remove the pulp and seeds, and dice the flesh into perfect little squares or *brunoise*.

Brush the bottom of a heaving frying pan with softened (not melted) butter. Cover the bottom with the shallots, parsley, and tomato *brunoise*.

Place the filets in the pan on top of the vegetables. Pour the fish stock over the filets. The stock should just cover them.

Cook on medium heat. When the stock begins to simmer, count approximately 4 minutes. Remove the filets and place on a warm serving dish.

Reduce the stock and vegetables in the same pan until the stock thickens slightly. Pour sauce over filets before serving.

—

Serves 4. Prep time: 20 minutes. Cook time: 10 minutes.

DESSERT

FRESH SEASONAL FRUIT

Poached in a Verbena Syrup with Salty Butter Cookies and Sweet Wine Sabayon

---

Fruit

3 pieces fresh seasonal fruit (such as pears, apples, quinces, peaches, or nectarines)

7 ounces (200 g) sugar

⅘ cup (20 cl) water

1 vanilla bean

12 fresh verbena leaves

Salted Butter Cookies

(makes 12 large cookies)

7¾ ounces (220g) flour

3/8 ounces (11 g) baking powder

1 vanilla bean

2½ ounces (70 g) granulated sugar

2½ ounces (70 g) cane sugar

5½ fl. ounces (160 g) salted butter

4 egg yolks

1¾ ounces (50 g) hazelnut powder

Sabayon

6 egg yolks

4¼ ounces (120 g) vanilla sugar

1 cup (25 cl) sweet white wine (Marsala, Sauternes, Rivesvalte, Pineau des Charentes)

The verbena syrup and fruit can be made ahead of time and kept in the refrigerator. The butter cookie dough may be made three days ahead and kept in the refrigerator. Bake the butter cookies in the morning and keep them in a closed container.

FRUIT. Peel and core the fruit. Add the sugar, water, and vanilla bean (cut in two); bring to a boil. Add the verbena leaves and let simmer a few minutes until all the sugar is dissolved. The longer the vanilla and verbena infuse, the more taste the syrup will have. Add the fruit and continue cooking approximately 30 minutes until fruit is cooked through but still somewhat firm. Let the fruit cool down in the syrup.

COOKIES. Sift the flour and baking powder together and set aside. Open the vanilla bean, remove grains with the tip of a knife, and rub the vanilla beans into the sugar. Using an electric mixer, mix the sugars and salted butter; then add egg yolks and hazelnut powder and mix thoroughly. Add the flour mixture all at once and mix just enough to incorporate.

Flatten out the dough into a disc shape, cover in plastic wrap, and place in refrigerator at least 30 minutes. Roll out the dough to about ½-inch thick and cut out perfect circles using a cookie cutter. Bake at 320°F (160°C) about 10 to 12 minutes.

SABAYON. Pour the ingredients into a round mixing bowl and place over a large pan of simmering water. Using a hand mixer, whisk the mixture briskly over the water bath for approximately 8 minutes. The sabayon should become very frothy as the egg yolks thicken. The sabayon should double in volume, and then whip another 30 seconds. Serve warm over the fruit and butter cookie.

———

Serves 6. Prep time: 45 minutes. Cook time for fruit: 30 minutes. Cook time for cookies: 12 minutes. Cook time for saboyan: 5 minutes.

MENU 05

SATURDAY NIGHT DINNERS—
MEAT LOVERS' SPECIAL

Appetizers

Beef Tenderloin with Arugula and Horseradish
Cream

Classic Beef Tartar with Capers, Onions, and Italian
Parsley

Main Course

Côte de Boeuf with Roasted Red Potatoes and
Beurre Maître d' Hôtel

Dessert

Plum and Fig Fruit Compote with Goat Milk Ice
Cream and Cocoa Nib Tuiles

This menu is all about red, juicy meat—some raw, some roasted. For meat lovers, there's nothing more satisfying than a nice piece of aged beef, perfectly cooked and well seasoned. Mastering the cooking of meat is not all that difficult; just follow these simple steps:

1. Remove meat from refrigerator 30 minutes before cooking; it should be nearly at room temperature.

2. Use fine salt to season the raw meat before cooking, then season with sea salt and black pepper after roasting.

3. Sear the meat first in hot oil (olive or grapeseed) on all sides, then add a nob of fresh butter and baste.

4. Finish roasting in a medium oven (350°F/180°C). For rare beef, count approximately 10 minutes per pound (500g).

5. Let rest before slicing for at least half of the cooking time.

Your carnivorous friends will be licking their chops!

APPETIZER

BEEF TENDERLOIN

with Arugula and Horseradish Cream

---

1 pound (500 g) beef tenderloin

about ⅓ cup (80 g) horseradish

2 tablespoons (30 g) crème fraiche

fresh arugula

fleur de sel

Place the tenderloin in the freezer for approximately 15 minutes. Cut into thin slices with a sharp chef's knife. Whisk the horseradish with the crème fraiche. Spread a thin layer of cream over one side of the slices. Add arugula leaves and roll tightly. Sprinkle with fleur de sel and keep refrigerated until ready to serve.

—

Serves 4. Prep time: 20 minutes.

APPETIZER

CLASSIC BEEF TARTAR

with Capers, Onions, and Italian Parsley

Beef

1 pound (500 g) tender beef ("tranche grasse")

1 shallot

2 spring onions

1 preserved lemon

½ bunch Italian parsley

Vinaigrette

juice of 1 lemon

Tabasco

Worcestershire sauce

6 tablespoons olive oil

2 organic egg yolks

2 tablespoons (30 g) small capers

sea salt, pepper

TARTAR. For this recipe, choose a tender cut of beef but not necessarily the filet. Many other tender cuts are also very flavorful. I like the *tranche grasse*. Ask your butcher for advice. The meat will be cut with a sharp knife and not ground; the taste will be even better this way.

Place the beef in the freezer for 15 minutes. This will make it easier to cut.

Slice first in thin strips following the meat's grain and then into small cubes. Keep refrigerated.

Peel and dice the shallot. Rinse and thinly slice the spring onions. Slice the preserved lemon in quarters, remove the pulp and seeds; slice rind into small cubes. Wash and mince the parsley.

VINAIGRETTE. Whisk the lemon juice, a few drops of Tabasco and Worcestershire sauce, and then the olive oil. Add all condiments to the beef, mix. Add vinaigrette and mix. Crack the eggs, separate the yolks from the whites. Rinse the eggshells, dry, and fill with egg yolks.

SERVE. Present the tartar on a large serving dish with egg yolks on top. Sprinkle with capers, sea salt, and fresh ground black pepper.

Serves 4. Prep time: 20 minutes.

MAIN COURSE

CÔTE DE BOEUF

with Roasted Red Potatoes and Beurre Maître d'Hôtel

Beurre Maître d'Hotel

½ pound (250 g) sweet
butter

1 clove garlic

½ bunch Italian parsley

½ bunch cilantro

½ bunch chives

fleur de sel

Red Potatoes

2¼ pounds (1kg) small
red potatoes

about ⅔ fl. ounces (20 g)
salted butter

2 tablespoons olive oil

2 spring onions

BEURRE MAÎTRE D'HÔTEL. Soften the butter using a spatula. Peel and mince the garlic. Wash, dry, and mince the fresh herbs. Add to butter, mixing thoroughly with the spatula. Place softened, seasoned butter onto a rectangular piece of plastic wrap. Roll butter into sausage shape with a 1-inch diameter and refrigerate until ready for use.

RED POTATOES. If necessary, brush the new potatoes but do not remove skin. Heat salted butter and olive oil until frothy in a heavy casserole dish. Add the potatoes and mix gently to coat them in the frothy butter. Continue roasting on medium heat. Rinse and slice the spring onions. After approximately 10 minutes, add the spring onions, mix, and lower heat. Cover and continue roasting 10 to 15 minutes. Season with sea salt. Potatoes should be slightly caramelized on the outside and tender inside. Keep warm.

Côte de Boeuf

1 aged côte de boeuf (2½ pounds (1.2 kg))

sea salt, pepper

2 tablespoons salted butter

2 tablespoons olive oil

Tips from a Pro

Nowadays, the trend is toward eating less meat. If you are a meat lover, then you should only use the best you can get. Talk to your butcher, explain to him what you want to make, and trust him to give you worthy advice.

CÔTE DE BOEUF. Preheat oven to 350°F (180°C). Remove the beef from the refrigerator at least 30 minutes before roasting. The meat must be nearly room temperature before cooking.

Heat 2 tablespoons of olive oil in an ovenproof skillet, and season the côte de boeuf on both sides with fine salt. Brown the beef on one side, approximately 4 to 5 minutes, turn over using tongs. Do not prick the beef with a fork, it will lose its juice.

Brown the other side approximately 2 minutes, add a good tablespoon of salted butter, and when it becomes frothy, baste the beef using a spoon, and cook another 2 minutes. This will help caramelize the meat. Browning the beef before roasting in the oven will ensure that the precious, flavorful juices stay in the meat. Place the skillet in the preheated oven. Roast for 15 minutes. The côte de boeuf should be served rare for best flavor.

Remove to a wire rack, cover with aluminum foil, and let rest at least 10 minutes. Letting the meat rest before slicing will allow the juices to spread through, making the meat much more tender. Roasting the meat with the bone in will always give more flavor.

Remove the bone with a sharp knife and slice the beef in 1-inch-thick slices. Serve warm.

—

Serves 4. Prep time: 20 minutes. Cook time: approximately 20 minutes.

DESSERT

PLUM AND FIG FRUIT COMPOTE

with Goat Milk Ice Cream and Cocoa Nib Tuiles

Goat Milk Ice Cream

1 quart (1 l) goat milk

2 vanilla beans

10 egg yolks

8.8 ounces (250 g) sugar

Compote

2¼ pounds (1 kg) red or purple plums

1 pound (500 g) figs

2¾ ounces (75 g) cane sugar

1 teaspoon (4 g) cinnamon

1 teaspoon (4 g) ground cardamom

Cocoa Nib Tuiles

(makes 30)

2 juice oranges

8.8 ounces (250 g) powdered sugar

1¾ ounces (50 g) flour

3½ fl. ounces (100 g) butter, melted

¾ ounces (20 g) cocoa nibs

¾ ounces (20 g) cocoa powder

ICE CREAM. Heat the goat milk with the seeds from the vanilla bean just to a boil in a saucepan. In a medium mixing bowl, whisk the egg yolks and sugar until the yolks become frothy and lighten in color. Pour the hot goat's milk over the egg yolks, whisk, and pour back into the saucepan. Heat to just before boiling; the mixture will thicken slightly and should coat the spoon. Pour into a clean mixing bowl and cool. Pour the mixture into the ice cream maker and churn until creamy. Keep in freezer until ready to serve. Homemade ice cream will always be creamier than the store-bought version.

FRUIT COMPOTE. Wash the fruit. Cut the plums in half and remove the pits. Cut the figs and plums in quarters. Place all the fruit in a large saucepan. Add the sugar, cinnamon, and cardamom, mix gently, and stew at medium heat approximately 20 minutes until fruit has rendered its juice. Remove to a serving bowl and let cool.

COCOA NIB TUILES. Preheat oven to 400°F (210°C). Juice the two oranges (about ½ cup/10 cl). Whisk the orange juice, powdered sugar, and flour. Mix well and then add the melted butter, the cocoa nibs, and the cocoa powder. Mix gently.

Cover a baking sheet with parchment paper or a nonstick baking mat. Spoon out a small amount of tuile batter and spread into a small circular shape. Leave space between each tuile; they spread out when baking. Bake for 10 minutes. Let the tuiles cool before removing to a wire rack. I like to leave them in a circular shape because they look like lace. You may give them a curved shape by placing the round tuiles on a rolling pin while still warm. Let cool then remove to a rack to continue cooling.

—

Compote and Ice Cream: Serves 4. Prep time: 40 minutes. Cook time: 27 minutes.

Cocoa Nib Tuiles: Prep time: 20 minutes. Cook time: 10 minutes.

MENU 06

SATURDAY NIGHT DINNERS—
AUTUMN HARVEST

Appetizers

Cream of Rutabaga Soup with White Truffle Oil
and Fresh Mushroom Crostini

Two-Texture Endive Salad with Toasted Hazelnuts
and Oranges and Hazelnut Oil Vinaigrette

Main Course

Allspice Roasted Duck Breast with Bitter Orange
Duck Jus and Potato Purée in Rosemary Butter

Dessert

Pecan Tartlet and Whipped Cream with
Gingerbread Spices

Fig and Red Grape Galette

Autumn is one of those special culinary seasons. The end of the summer produce, still abundant and fully ripened, sits right alongside the first root vegetables, vibrant orange squash, and woody, fresh mushrooms. The fruit is a rich, deep violet in color, and figs, plums, and Muscat grapes abound. The cooler weather spikes our appetite, and this satisfying menu is sure to please the whole table.

APPETIZER

CREAM OF RUTABAGA SOUP

with White Truffle Oil and Fresh Mushroom Crostini

Soup

1¼ cups (300 g) rutabaga

1 sweet white onion

about ⁴/₅ fl. ounces (25 g) salted butter

salt, pepper

2 cups (50 cl) vegetable stock, warm

white truffle oil

1 good quality baguette

olive oil

Mushrooms

about ¾ cups (200 g) wild, seasonal mushrooms (chanterelles, portobello, black trumpet)

1 shallot

olive oil

1 teaspoon salted butter

white truffle oil

—

Tips from a Pro

Most mushrooms may be cleaned simply with a damp brush; never leave them to soak in water—they are like sponges! When sautéing mushrooms, salt after they render their natural liquids. This will keep them from becoming soggy.

SOUP. Peel and slice the rutabaga and the sweet onion. Heat the butter in a large saucepan until frothy. Add the sliced onions and heat through to sweat. Season with salt and pepper. Add the sliced rutabaga and mix to slightly coat with the frothy butter. Cover with warmed vegetable stock, bring to a boil, lower the heat, and simmer for approximately 20 minutes until rutabaga is tender. Remove the vegetables to a blender using a slotted spoon. Add a little cooking liquid and blend to a smooth, creamy texture. Add more liquid if needed. Pour into a medium saucepan, check the seasoning, and keep warm.

Slice the baguette in approximately ½-inch-thick slices. Brush with olive oil on both sides and toast in a 350°F (180°) oven for 10 minutes.

MUSHROOMS. Fill a salad bowl with cool water and quickly submerge the chanterelles and black trumpet mushrooms. Swirl them in the water and remove immediately, using your hands to sift. Place on a clean towel and pat dry. The portobellos should be cleaned with a damp brush and not submerged in water or they will become spongy.

Cut all mushrooms in two or four. Peel and finely slice the shallot. Heat a little olive oil in a heavy frying pan and sweat the shallot until soft. Add the mushrooms and sauté until they lose their natural liquid. Add 1 teaspoon of salted butter, season with salt and pepper, and let brown slightly. Remove to absorbent paper.

SERVE. Spread the mushrooms on the toasted baguette. Heat the cream of rutabaga soup, add a few drops of white truffle oil, and top with mushroom crostini. Serve warm.

—

Serves 4. Prep time: 20 minutes. Cook time: 15 minutes.

APPETIZER

TWO-TEXTURE ENDIVE SALAD

with Toasted Hazelnuts and Oranges and Hazelnut Oil Vinaigrette

---

Endive Salad

5 white endives

about ⅔ fl. ounces (20 g) sweet butter

salt, pepper

juice of 1 orange

about ¼ cup (50 g) toasted hazelnuts

3 oranges

hazelnut oil

white balsamic vinegar

Vinaigrette

juice of ½ orange

2 tablespoons white balsamic vinegar

salt, pepper

sea salt or fleur de sel

3 tablespoons olive oil

3 tablespoons hazelnut oil

small head red-speckled lettuce

ENDIVE SALAD. Rinse the endives. Cut them in two lengthwise and remove the core. Slice three of them thinly. Set the two others aside.

Heat the butter in a heavy frying pan until frothy. Add the sliced endives. Coat in the butter and heat through gently until endives have wilted. Season with salt and pepper. Add half of the fresh orange juice and continue heating until orange juice has reduced. Remove endive to absorbent paper.

Slice the remaining endive in two lengthwise and remove the core. Slice them in ¾ inch slices at an angle. Keep chilled.

Toast the hazelnuts in a hot frying pan without any oil. Rotate the pan regularly to toast the hazelnuts on all sides. When toasted (about 4 minutes), transfer to a cutting board and chop into small pieces using a chef's knife.

Peel the oranges using a paring knife to be sure to remove the pith.

Supreme the oranges (remove the wedges by cutting on either side of the white sections). Slice the wedges in 2 equal pieces.

VINAIGRETTE. Whisk ingredients together, finishing with the two oils.

SERVE. Place a small circle of the endive compote in the center of a small salad plate. Cover with slices of fresh endive and leaves of red-speckled lettuce. Place 3 orange segments, sprinkle with toasted hazelnuts, and season well with the vinaigrette. Sprinkle the top with sea salt. Serve.

Serves 4. Prep time: 15 minutes. Cook time: 15 minutes.

MAIN COURSE

ALLSPICE ROASTED DUCK BREAST

with Bitter Orange Duck Jus and Potato Purée in Rosemary Butter

Duck

2 duck breasts

1 heaping teaspoon (6 g) allspice

salt, pepper

12 red grapes, 12 green grapes

Duck Jus

about ⁴/₅ cups (200 g) duck meat from the thigh

1 sweet onion

1 carrot

juice of 1 bitter orange

½ fl. ounce (15 g) grapeseed oil

about ⁴/₅ fl. ounce (25 g) sweet butter

2 cups (50 cl) veal stock

Potato Purée in Rosemary Butter

1½ pounds (600 g) russet potatoes or bintje

about ⁴/₅ cups (200 g) whole milk

6¾ fl. ounces (200 g) salted butter

3 sprigs fresh rosemary

sea salt, fresh pepper

DUCK. Preheat oven to 350°F (180°). Remove the excess fat so it just covers the meat. Using a sharp paring knife, score the fat, but not the meat, in a diamond pattern. Season well on both sides with the allspice, salt, and pepper.

Heat a heavy ovenproof skillet without oil or butter. Place the duck breast in the hot skillet, fat side down. Let brown thoroughly; this will take approximately 4 to 5 minutes. Remove the rendered fat, keeping 1 tablespoon, turn the duck over (fat side up), and place skillet in preheated oven for 12 minutes. The duck meat will be rare or rosé—the best way to eat duck. Overcooking it will toughen the meat.

Remove the breast to a rack and cover with aluminum foil for at least 5 minutes to allow the meat to rest before slicing. If you slice right out of the oven, the juices will escape! Don't let them get away; they're too delicious! Keep the meat warm by putting it back into the warm oven, but turn off the heat.

In a small frying pan, heat up the tablespoon of rendered fat and add the grapes. Let them just heat through. Keep warm.

DUCK JUS. Slice the duck meat into small pieces. Peel and dice the onion; peel and dice the carrot. Juice the orange. Heat the grapeseed oil in a medium saucepan. Add the duck meat and brown for approximately 5 minutes. Add the butter and continue browning for 10 minutes.

The meat should be nearly caramelized. Add the diced vegetables and continue browning another 6 minutes. Add a bit more butter if necessary.

Remove all the meat and vegetables with a slotted spoon. Deglaze the meat juices with a bit of cold water by scraping the bottom of the pan with the slotted spoon. Put meat and vegetables back into the pan, and

Tips from a Pro

This is a great dish for dinner parties because you can brown the duck breasts before your guests arrive, set them aside, and then finish cooking in the oven just before going to the table.

add the bitter orange juice and the veal stock. Bring to a boil then reduce and simmer for at least 1 hour.

Strain the liquid into a smaller saucepan using a fine strainer. Heat and let reduce by a third. Add a teaspoon of sweet butter and whisk briskly to finish sauce. Season with salt and pepper if needed. Keep warm.

POTATO PUREE. Peel the potatoes and place in a large pot of cold water. Bring to a boil and add sea salt. Cook until tender, about 20 minutes. Heat the milk, butter, and rosemary in a small saucepan. Let the rosemary infuse for approximately 15 minutes on low heat.

Strain the potatoes. Pass through a stainless steel food mill. For perfectly smooth and light purée, pass through a fine sieve using a rubber scraper. Put the fine purée back into the pot and pour in the butter and milk mixture (without the rosemary sprig). Whip gently until all the milk has been absorbed. Add more butter if necessary. Check seasoning. Keep warm.

SERVE. Slice the warm duck into ½-inch slices at an angle. On a warmed plate, add a swirl of potato purée, place the duck seasoned with a little sea salt, and add a nice curved line of duck jus. Finish with the warm grapes and serve immediately.

—

Serves 4. Prep time: 30 minutes. Cook time: 1 hour 20 minutes.

DESSERT

PECAN TARTLET

and Whipped Cream with Gingerbread Spices

Sweet Dough

3¼ fl. ounces (95 g) sweet butter

1 ounce (30) g almond powder

¼ teaspoon (1 g) salt

3¼ ounces (90 g) powdered sugar

1¾ ounces (50 g) potato starch (to give the dough more elasticity)

6¾ ounces (180 g) flour

1⅘ fl. ounces (55 g) egg

Pecan Filling

3 eggs

4.4 ounces (125 g) sugar

½ teaspoon salt

2½ fl. ounces (75 g) melted butter

4¼ fl. ounces (125 g) pure maple syrup

about ½ cup (125 g) pecans

Whipped Cream

17 fl. ounces (50 cl) whipping cream

1¼ ounces (35 g) powdered sugar

2 teaspoons (8 g) gingerbread spices (ginger, cinnamon, allspice, cloves, nutmeg)

DOUGH. Using a mixer and the paddle attachment, mix the butter until softened. Sift all of the dry ingredients except the flour together, add to butter, and mix well. Add ⅓ of the eggs and ⅓ of the flour. Mix well. Continue by thirds until all of the eggs and flour are mixed. Remove the dough, shape into a flattened disc, cover in plastic wrap, and refrigerate overnight.

Preheat oven to 375°F (190°C). Roll out the dough to ¼-inch thick. Using a round cookie cutter cut out 4 discs. Butter the molds and refrigerate 10 minutes.

Place discs of dough into the round molds and affix the dough to the mold by pressing gently between thumb and fingertips. Refrigerate for 15 minutes. Place a round disc of parchment paper into each mold, fill with pie weights, and blind bake for 15 minutes. Remove to a rack to cool.

FILLING. Whisk all ingredients except pecans together. Break the pecans into halves and cover the bottom of each pie crust. Place the crusts onto a baking sheet. Fill the crusts ⅔ with the pecan filling. Bake for 20 minutes, the filling should be lightly browned and firm. Remove to a rack to cool.

WHIPPED CREAM. Place the cream in a mixing bowl and place it in the refrigerator for 15 minutes. Using a mixer, whip the cream slowly at first. Increase the speed little by little so that the cream emulsifies and becomes stiff. Once stiff, add the powdered sugar and whip gently. Add the spices and whip just until blended. Remove the cream to a pastry bag with a small round tip and keep refrigerated.

SERVE. When pecan tartlets are fully cooled, decorate with rounds of whipped cream and a sprinkle of spices. The tartlets may be refrigerated several hours.

—

4 individual tartlets. Prep time: 30 minutes. Cook time: 35 minutes.

DESSERT

FIG AND RED GRAPE GALETTE

1 circle of puff pastry, 9 inches (24 cms), pure butter

cane sugar

10 figs

20 red grapes

Preheat oven to 375°F (190°C). Place the circle of puff pastry onto a baking sheet covered in parchment paper. Roll up the edges approximately ¾ inches. Prick the bottom with a fork and sprinkle with cane sugar. Place in refrigerator for 15 minutes. Wash the figs and grapes.

Slice the figs in quarters. Arrange the figs in a circular pattern skin-side down. Add the red grapes between the figs. Sprinkle with cane sugar and bake for approximately 30 minutes. Puff pastry must be well-baked. It should be golden and crunchy. Serve warm.

—

Serves 6. Prep time: 15 minutes. Cook time: 30 minutes.

M E N U 0 7

A SWEET PRINCESS BIRTHDAY

Appetizers
Mini Pasta Salads in Shells

Croque Monsieur Finger Sandwiches with Swiss
Cheese Cream

Smoked Salmon and Cream Cheese California
Rolls

Rainbow Tomatoes and Feta Cheese Skewers

Dessert
Choux with Vanilla Pastry Cream and Sweet
Fondant

Vanilla, Strawberry, and Rose Praline Cupcakes

Mini Lemon Meringue Tarts

I had so much fun coming up with this menu. We all know that fairy tale princesses don't really exist, nor does the charming prince, but how wonderful it is to "make believe" every once and awhile. It's your little girl's birthday? Let her dream a bit and make everything pink!

It's a birthday party so there will of course be lots of sweets, but try to balance the menu a bit by proposing a few yummy savory bites, as well. Nothing but easy finger food sure to please any eight-year-old!

The pastry is basically the best of both worlds, sweet American cupcakes and light and airy French pate à chou. I've also thrown in wonderful lemon meringue tartlets, just about everyone's favorite.

"Bon anniversaire, Princesse!"

APPETIZER

MINI PASTA SALADS IN SHELLS

18 pasta shells (lumaconi or conchiglie)

1 zucchini

1 red pepper

1 yellow pepper

1 orange pepper

3 tablespoons olive oil

sea salt, pepper

1 bunch small-leaf basil

Cook the pasta shells in a large quantity of boiling salted water to al dente. The shells should be firm, as they will become the pasta bowls. Drain and place on a plate, drizzle with a little olive oil, and let cool.

Wash all vegetables. Slice zucchini in small cubes (*brunoise*). Cut the peppers in two, remove the heart and seeds and dice peppers in the same size cubes as the zucchini (*brunoise*).

Heat olive oil in a heavy skillet and sauté the zucchini and peppers until tender. Season with sea salt and pepper. Add a few basil leaves and heat through.

Fill each pasta shell with a spoonful of vegetables. Add a few drops of olive oil and decorate with a leaf of fresh basil. Serve on a pretty platter.

—

Serves 6. Prep time: 20 minutes. Cook time: 18 minutes.

APPETIZER

CROQUE MONSIEUR FINGER SANDWICHES

with Swiss Cheese Cream

12 slices good bread (in France, I buy fresh *pain de mie* at the bakery and have it sliced)

17 fl. ounces (50 cl) crème fraiche or heavy cream

about ⅔ cup (150 g) freshly grated Swiss cheese

1 whole nutmeg, grated

6 slices ham, braised

6 slices Swiss cheese

about ¼ cup (50g) freshly grated parmesan

This is the Palace hotel version of the croque monsieur. Instead of the béchamel, I use thick Swiss cheese cream, a bit quicker but richer and so delicious!

Mix the crème fraiche with the grated Swiss cheese. Season with freshly grated nutmeg. Place the slices of fresh bread on a baking sheet. Spread both sides of the bread with the Swiss cheese cream. Add a slice of good, braised ham, a slice of Swiss cheese, and cover with the second piece of bread. Cover the top with freshly grated parmesan and bake in a 390°F (200°C) oven for approximately 8 to 10 minutes. Top should be lightly browned and bubbly.

Let cool and slice into long strips.

Serve piled up, similar to the game Jenga. The little girls will love these finger sandwiches. Have plenty of small napkins available—no forks and knives today!

—

Serves 6. Prep time: 20 minutes. Cook time: 10 minutes.

APPETIZER

SMOKED SALMON AND CREAM CHEESE CALIFORNIA ROLLS

Filling

2 cups sushi or short grain rice

1⅔ cups (40 cl) cold water, plus extra for rinsing rice

2 tablespoons rice vinegar

2 tablespoons sugar

1 tablespoon sea salt

Sushi Rolls

2 carrots

1 small cucumber

4 slices smoked salmon

4 sheets nori

1¼ cups (300 g) softened cream cheese

½ batch sushi rice

⅓ cup black sesame seeds, toasted

Wasabi, for serving

Sweet soy sauce, for serving

FILLING: Sushi rice needs to be thoroughly rinsed. Place the rice into a mixing bowl and cover with cool water. Swirl the rice in the water, pour off, and repeat 2 to 3 times or until the water is clear.

Place the rice and measured cold water into a medium saucepan and place over high heat. Bring to a boil, uncovered. Once it begins to boil, reduce the heat to the lowest setting and cover. Cook for 15 minutes. Remove from the heat and let stand, covered, for 10 minutes.

Combine the rice vinegar, sugar, and salt in a small saucepan and heat through until sugar melts. Transfer the rice into a large wooden dish with a flat bottom. The traditional dish is called a hangiri. Add the vinegar mixture to the rice, folding thoroughly to combine and coat each grain of rice with the mixture. Let cool to room temperature before using.

ROLLS: California rolls usually have avocado in them; I guess that's why they're called California rolls. I don't use them for the little girls—avocado is not usually one of their favorites. I use carrots and cucumbers instead.

Peel the carrots and cucumber. Cut cucumber in two lengthwise and remove the seeds. Slice into thin strips. Slice the carrot into the same size strips. Slice the smoked salmon into strips, as well.

Lay out a bamboo sushi mat. Cover it with plastic wrap. Place a nori sheet on the plastic wrap. Spread the cream cheese over the entire surface. Wet your fingers and spread a layer of sushi rice. Using the plastic wrap, turn the nori sheet over and remove the wrap. The rice side is now down on the mat.

Place strips of carrots, cucumber, and salmon along the entire width. Using mat, roll tightly. If needed, wet your fingers to prevent the rice from sticking. Roll the rice side in black sesame seeds, cover with a damp cloth, and keep in refrigerator. Keep rolling until all the rice has been used.

When ready to serve, cut each roll into 6 pieces and serve with sweet soy sauce and a pinch of wasabi.

—

Serves 6. Prep time: 30 minutes. Cook time: 25 minutes (15 cooking, 10 resting).

APPETIZER

RAINBOW TOMATOES AND FETA CHEESE SKEWERS

18 red cherry tomatoes

18 orange cherry tomatoes

18 yellow cherry tomatoes

about ⅘ cup (200 g) Greek feta cheese

Chives

Sea salt

Olive oil

This is very simple and delicious. The girls would enjoy making them themselves.

Rinse the tomatoes. Cut the feta into medium-sized cubes. Alternate the tomatoes on a bamboo skewer and finish with a cube of feta. Tie a chive around the skewer at the bottom. Sprinkle with sea salt and a few drops of olive oil.

—

Serves 6. Prep time: 15 minutes.

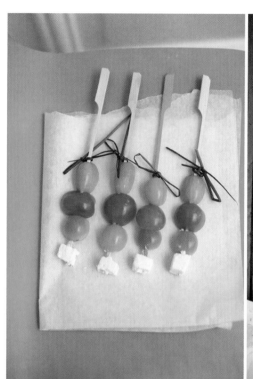

DESSERT

CHOUX

with Vanilla Pastry Cream and Sweet Fondant

Craquelin *or Crunchy Topping*

about 2.5 tablespoons (40 g) soft, salted butter

1¾ ounces (50 g) brown sugar

1¾ ounces (50 g) flour

Pâte à Chou

½ cup (125 g) whole milk

½ cup (125 g) water

3½ fl. ounces (100 g) butter

2 teaspoons (8 g) sugar

⅔ teaspoon (4 g) salt

½ cup (125 g) flour

4 whole eggs

CRAQUELIN. Mix all ingredients together using a mixer with the paddle attachment. Remove dough and form into a flat disc shape. Roll out between two pieces of parchment paper. The dough should be less than ¼-inch thick. Using a small round cookie cutter, the size of the cream puffs, mark the dough with circles, without cutting all the way through. Place the dough on a baking sheet and place in freezer for at least 2 hours, and ideally, overnight.

PÂTE À CHOU. Preheat convection oven to 350°F (180°C). Heat the milk, water, butter, sugar, and salt in a medium saucepan, just to boiling. Remove from heat and add the flour all at once. Mix briskly with a wooden spatula. Put the saucepan back on the heat and continue stirring briskly. At this point, there should be no more lumps, the dough should be smooth and start forming a ball. Continue heating to fully dry out the dough. The process will take approximately 5 minutes.

Remove the dough to a clean mixing bowl. Break the eggs into a small bowl. Add one egg at a time to the dough mixture. Mix briskly with a wooden spatula until the entire egg is thoroughly blended. Do the same with the 3 other eggs. The dough should form soft peaks.

Prepare a pastry bag with a small round tip; fill with the *pâte à chou*. Cover a baking sheet with parchment paper. Pipe out the dough in small, regular-sized balls, the size of small apricots.

Remove the *craquelin* dough from freezer. Cut through the circles using the round cookie cutter. Delicately place a circle of *craquelin* on top of each ball of dough.

Bake in convection oven, no more than 2 baking sheets at a time, for 25 to 30 minutes. The *chou* should be golden brown and fully baked through. They will feel very light. If the *chou* are not baked thoroughly, the steam inside will make them fall. Remove to a rack to cool.

Vanilla Pastry Cream

1 vanilla bean

4 egg yolks

3½ ounces (100 g) sugar

1.4 ounces (40 g) corn-
starch

1 cup (25 cl) fresh whole
milk

about 3⅓ tablespoons (50
g) fresh butter

Sweet Fondant or Glace
Royale

1 egg white

juice of ½ lemon

5.3 ounces (150 g)
powdered sugar

pink and red food
coloring pigments

VANILLA PASTRY CREAM. Open the vanilla pod and scrape out the seeds using the tip of a knife. Place egg yolks, sugar, and vanilla into a medium mixing bowl. Whip the mixture briskly by hand. It will lighten in color. Add the cornstarch and whip briskly to thoroughly mix.

Heat the milk in a medium saucepan; bring to boil and pour the hot milk onto the egg mixture. Mix and pour back into the saucepan. Mix continually using the whip until the pastry cream thickens, about 2 minutes. Bring just to a boil and pour the cream into a clean mixing bowl. Whip the fresh, softened butter briskly into the pastry cream.

Let cool by placing the mixing bowl into an ice bath. Prepare a pastry bag with a small round tip. Once cooled, fill the pastry bag with the pastry cream and place in refrigerator until ready to use. Pastry cream does not freeze well and should be used very fresh.

SWEET FONDANT. Place the egg white in a stainless steel mixing bowl. Add the lemon juice. This will keep the icing white and help it to dry faster. Sift the powdered sugar and add half to the egg whites. Whisk briskly and add the rest of the powdered sugar. Check the consistency. If needed, add more powdered sugar to thicken.

Split the icing into three separate bowls and, using a small spatula, color each to different hues of pink.

FILLING AND ICING THE *CHOUX*. When fully cooled, make a small hole in the bottom of each *chou* using a small star tip. Place the tip of the vanilla cream pastry bag into the hole and press gently, filling the *chou* until the cream shows. Wipe the excess. Dip the top of the *chou* into the desired colored icing, wipe off excess icing. Decorate with colored sugar or candied rose petals. Filled *chou* may be refrigerated for a few hours but should be consumed the same day. They are so delicious when fresh, believe me, you won't want to store them for long!

Makes approximately 24 small cream puffs. Prep time: 20 minutes. Cook time: 30 to 35 minutes.

DESSERT

VANILLA, STRAWBERRY, AND ROSE PRALINE CUPCAKES

Cupcake Base

3.88 ounces (110 g) sweet butter at room temperature

8 ounces (225 g) cane sugar

2 organic eggs

9.7 ounces (275 g) flour

⅓ ounce (11 g) baking powder

½ cup (12 cl) fresh whole milk, room temperature

Vanilla Cupcakes

Base +

1 teaspoon good quality vanilla extract

Strawberry Cupcakes

Base +

4 tablespoons strawberry purée

12 fresh strawberries

Rose Cupcakes

Base +

1 tablespoon rose water

pink pralines, for decoration

CUPCAKE BASE. (If making Strawberry Cupcakes, wash and slice strawberries lengthwise.)

Place the butter and sugar in the mixer. Using the paddle attachment, mix briskly, approximately 5 minutes. The mixture should lighten in color and become very smooth. Add the eggs one by one, mixing thoroughly. Sift the flour and baking powder together in a small mixing bowl. Mix the milk and vanilla extract (or strawberry puree, or rose water) together in a jug. Add ⅓ of the flour mixture to the egg mixture, then ⅓ of the milk. Mix well. Continue adding the flour mixture then milk mixture by thirds until well blended.

Preheat oven to 320°F (160°C). Prepare muffin tins with paper cupcake liners. Fill cups ⅔ full (insert strawberry halves here if making strawberry cupcakes) and bake for 25 minutes. Remove to rack to cool.

Plain Buttercream

1 whole egg

4.4 ounces (125 g) sugar

8.8 ounces (250 g) sweet
butter, room temperature

1 teaspoon of desired
flavor: pure vanilla
extract, rose water, coffee,
pistachio paste, etc.

pigment-based food
coloring

BUTTERCREAM. Add whole egg and sugar to a stainless steel mixing bowl. Place on top of a medium saucepan, ⅓ full of water to create a water bath. Water should be simmering. Whisk continually by hand or using an electric hand mixer. The mixture should lighten in color and become very frothy and light, nearly doubling in volume.

When the mixture has reached the right consistency and has warmed, remove from water bath and continue mixing to cool. It is important that the egg mixture be cool before adding the butter.

Mix in the softened butter little by little. The butter mustn't separate from the egg mixture. Once all the butter is added, continue mixing at least one minute. Add the desired flavor and color at this point and whip thoroughly.

Remove buttercream to a pastry bag with the desired tip (round or star). Keep refrigerated until ready for use. The buttercream may be frozen, but before use, whip briskly to lighten up.

———

For Cupcakes: Makes 12 large cupcakes or 24 small. Prep time: 20 minutes. Cook time: 25 minutes for large, 16 minutes for small.

Makes enough buttercream for 12 cupcakes. Prep time: 20 minutes. Cook time: 10 minutes.

DESSERT

MINI LEMON MERINGUE TARTS

Sweet Dough

3¼ fl. ounces (95 g) sweet butter

1 ounce (30 g) almond powder

1¾ ounces (50 g) potato starch (to give the dough more elasticity)

salt

3.7 ounces (90 g) powdered sugar

1⅘ fl. ounces (55 g) egg

6.34 ounces (180 g) flour

Lemon Cream

zest of 2 organic lemons

7 ounces (200 g) sugar

⅔ cup (16 cl) lemon juice (approx. 3 lemons)

4 eggs

7 ounces (200 g) sweet butter, room temperature

SWEET DOUGH. Make the dough the day before; it will be so much easier to work with after a night in the refrigerator. Using a mixer and the paddle attachment, mix the butter until softened. Sift all of the dry ingredients, except the flour, together, add to butter and mix well. Add ⅓ of the eggs and ⅓ of the flour. Mix well. Continue by thirds until all the eggs and flour are mixed. Remove the dough, shape into a flattened disc, cover in plastic wrap, and refrigerate overnight.

LEMON CREAM. Zest the 2 organic lemons using a fine grater (microplane), into the sugar. Add sugar, eggs, and lemon juice to a stainless steel mixing bowl. Place onto a medium saucepan filled ⅓ with water to make a water bath. Water should be simmering. Whisk briskly. The mix will thicken as the eggs cook through. Cook to 183°F (84°C), and check temperature using a pastry thermometer.

Remove mixing bowl and let lemon cream cool down to 95°F (35°C). Mix in the softened butter using a hand blender. Remove to pastry bag with a small, round tip. Keep refrigerated until ready for use.

French Meringue

5 egg whites (150 g), room temperature

4.4 ounces (125 g) sugar

4.4 ounces (125 g) powdered sugar

edible flowers

—

These tarts are easy enough that the children can help with them—this is what makes them so much fun. They'll certainly enjoy it more!

FOR THE FRENCH MERINGUE. Whip egg whites until frothy. Add the sugar little by little and continue whipping until egg whites are firm and shiny. Add the powdered sugar all at once and whip gently to mix. Remove meringue to a pastry bag with a small round tip. Keep refrigerated until ready for use.

BLIND BAKE THE SWEET DOUGH. Preheat oven to 350°F (175°C). Roll dough to a rectangular shape approximately ¼-inch thick. Cut out circles that match the size of your tartlet molds, using a cookie cutter. Butter the molds. Place dough circles gently into molds and press with fingertips. Prick the bottom of the dough and bake for 15 minutes. Remove sweet dough to rack to cool.

FILL AND DECORATE THE TARTLETS. Fill each tartlet with lemon cream using the pastry bag. Top with meringue and color the top using a blow torch (don't let the kids do this part unless they're well supervised!). Decorate with edible flowers such as pansies.

—

Makes 24 tartlets. Prep time: 30 minutes. Resting time: 12 hours. Cooking time: 30 minutes.

Lemon cream: makes enough for 24 tartlets. Prep time: 20 minutes. Cook time: 15 minutes.

M E N U   0 8

FIRESIDE APPETIZERS

Snacks

Sweet Bell Pepper and Cream
Cheese *Religieuse*

Parmesan Butter Biscuits and Red
Radish Dip

Root Vegetable Minestrone with
Parmesan Tuiles

Main Courses

Seared Sea Scallops with French
Lentils, Parma Ham Chips, and
Smoked Bacon Emulsion

Lightly Battered Deep-Fried Prawn
with Tartar Sauce

Beef Cubes Marinated in Sweet
Sake and Miso with Butternut
Squash Discs in Grapefruit and
Orange Reduction with Ginger

Free-Range Chicken Breast Bites
with Coconut, Turmeric, and Kaffir Leaf Grilled on an Open Fire

Cheese

Roquefort and Pear Puffs

Dessert

Individual-Sized Fresh Fruit Crumble
with Toasted Walnuts

Extra-Moist Chocolate Cake with
a Caramel Center

Praline and Chocolate Nib *Financiers*

Mini *Mont Blanc* Cakes

Y ou've invited lots of friends for a light weekend dinner and you're not too sure what time the guests will arrive, nor exactly how many friends, or friends of friends, will show up. You'd also really enjoy spending some time with them all, so you don't necessarily want to be in the kitchen the whole evening.

Gourmet dinner appetizers are my favorite delicious approach to these types of events. When I was a private chef, I often had requests for this type of meal; it makes for a very informal and relaxed way to entertain. I don't really like the idea of a buffet, where everything is put out on the table at the same time with no rhyme or reason. This menu is designed to be a complete, balanced meal and should be served in stages.

As the guests arrive, the gourmet snacks may be served. Next comes the warm appetizer followed by four main dishes featuring scrumptious marinated beef, lightly battered prawns, seared scallops, and Thai-style chicken.

In France, the cheese course is always important. For this menu, the cheese will be served warm and in individual portions. When all of the savory bites have been eaten up, it's time to bring on the desserts—a delectable selection of individual treats sure to please every sweet tooth.

The key here is to present the dishes in single serving plates or large platters, making serving and eating simpler. Ask a bartender friend to come up with amusing cocktails to accompany the dishes, make a fire in the fireplace, or light a campfire and simply enjoy!

SNACK

SWEET BELL PEPPER AND CREAM CHEESE *RELIGIEUSE*

Pâte à Chou

½ cup (125 g) whole milk

½ cup (125 g) water

3⅓ fl. ounces (100 g) butter

1 teaspoon (4 g) sugar

⅔ teaspoon (4 g) salt

½ cup (125 g) flour

4 whole eggs

Filling

2 roasted red peppers or piquillos, sliced

about ¾ cup (200 g) softened cream cheese

¼ cup (50 g) fresh cream

dill sprigs

Preheat convection oven to 350°F (180°C). Heat the milk, water, butter, sugar, and salt in a medium saucepan, just to boiling. Remove from heat and add the flour all at once. Mix briskly with a rubber spatula. Put the saucepan back on the heat and continue stirring briskly. At this point, there should be no more lumps, and the dough should be smooth and start forming a ball. Continue heating to fully dry out the dough. The process will take approximately 5 minutes. Remove the dough to a clean mixing bowl. Break the eggs into a small bowl. Add 1 egg at a time to the dough mixture. Mix briskly with a rubber spatula until the entire egg is thoroughly blended. Do the same with the 3 other eggs. The dough should form soft peaks.

Prepare two pastry bags: one with a small round tip, the second with a medium round tip. Fill both with the *pate à chou*. Cover a baking sheet with parchment paper. Pipe out the dough into small, regular-sized balls. Then, using the larger tip, pipe out into a bit larger-sized balls, the size of a small apricot. You will need the same number of both sizes.

Bake in a convection oven, no more than 2 baking sheets at a time, for 25 to 30 minutes. The *chou* should be golden brown and fully baked through. They will feel very light. If the "chou" are not baked thoroughly, the steam inside will make them fall. Remove to a wire rack to cool.

FILLING. Place the sliced roasted peppers in bowl of the food processor with the cream cheese and fresh cream. Mix to obtain a smooth, creamy texture. Remove to a pastry bag with a small round tip. Using a small star tip, poke a hole in the bottom of each of the *chou*. Fill with the red pepper cream. Pipe out a bit of cream on the larger *chou* and top with the smaller one. Pipe a dollop of cream on the top and decorate with a slice of pepper and a sprig of dill.

Makes 12 cream puffs. Prep time: 40 minutes. Cook time: 35 minutes.

SNACK

PARMESAN BUTTER BISCUITS AND RED RADISH DIP

Radish Dip

1 cucumber

12 red radishes

1 bunch of chives

about 2¼ cups (500 g) *fromage blanc* or thick Greek yogurt

juice of ½ lemon

1 clove garlic, green germ removed and finely minced

Salt, pepper

Biscuits

4 fl. ounces (120 g) butter

6.3 ounces (180 g) flour

¾ cup (180 g) freshly grated parmesan

½ teaspoon fleur de sel

1 egg

pepper

RADISH DIP. Peel cucumber, slice in half lengthwise, and remove seeds using a small spoon. Dice into small squares, or *brunoise*. Wash and slice the red radishes. Add the vegetables to the *fromage blanc*, add lemon juice, garlic, and season with salt and pepper. Mix gently and keep refrigerated until serving.

PARMESAN BISCUITS. Preheat oven to 350°F (180°C). Using the mixer with the paddle attachment, mix the butter, flour, parmesan, and fleur de sel. Add the egg and mix until dough forms a rough ball. Remove and place on a sheet of plastic wrap. Roll the dough in the plastic wrap to form a thin log. Place in refrigerator at least 1 hour. This dough may be made ahead and frozen.

Remove the dough and slice thinly. Prepare a baking tray with parchment paper or a nonstick baking mat. Bake for 8 minutes or until just golden. Remove to a rack to cool. Serve with the radish dip.

—

Makes approximately 30 biscuits. Prep time: 30 minutes. Cook time: 8 minutes.

SNACK

ROOT VEGETABLE MINESTRONE WITH PARMESAN TUILES

Minestrone

2 orange carrots

2 violet carrots

3 zucchini

½ head purple cauliflower

½ head yellow cauliflower

2 parsnips

3 tablespoons olive oil

sea salt

2 quarts (2 l) fresh chicken or vegetable stock

Parmesan Tuiles

about ¾ cup (200 g) freshly grated parmesan

This hearty soup may be prepared 2 days in advance and kept refrigerated.

MINESTRONE. Wash all vegetables. Peel the carrots and the parsnips. Dice all into small cubes or *macedoine*. Separate the cauliflower into small bouquets. Heat the olive oil in a large stockpot. Sweat all of the vegetables in the oil, coating them well. After about 5 minutes, season with sea salt. Cover in chicken or vegetable stock, bring to a boil, then reduce the heat and simmer for 40 minutes until all of the vegetables are cooked through. They should remain slightly firm. I prefer the all-seasonal vegetable version of minestrone, but to make it heartier, you may also add potatoes or small pasta. To develop more flavor, remove from heat and let cool a bit to infuse the vegetables in the stock. Reheat before serving.

PARMESAN TUILES. Place small mounds of freshly grated parmesan onto a nonstick baking mat on a baking sheet. Bake tuiles in a 350°F (180°C) oven for approximately 10 to 12 minutes. They should be slightly golden. Remove to a wire rack for cooling.

Serve with the piping hot minestrone.

—

Serves 6. Prep time: 40 minutes. Cook time: 45 minutes.

MAIN COURSE

SEARED SEA SCALLOPS

with French Lentils, Parma Ham Chips, and Smoked Bacon Emulsion

---

Lentils

1 carrot

1 sweet white onion

2 stalks celery

2 tablespoons olive oil

1¼ cup (300 g) French green lentils

2 quarts (2 l) cold water or vegetable stock

Salt, pepper

Parma Ham Chips

6 slices of Parma ham

Smoked Bacon Emulsion

about 8½ fl. ounces (250 g) heavy whipping cream

1¾ ounces (50 g) smoked bacon

LENTILS. Peel carrot and onion. Dice finely. Wash the celery and dice. In a large saucepan, sweat the vegetables in 2 tablespoons of olive oil. Add lentils and mix gently to coat with oil and vegetables. Cover with cold water or vegetable stock, bring to a boil, reduce heat, and let simmer for approximately 25 minutes. The lentils should be slightly firm. Do not salt during the cooking or the lentils will toughen. Strain the lentils, return to the saucepan, and season with salt and pepper.

PARMA HAM CHIPS. Preheat oven to 350°F (180°C). Cover a baking sheet with a nonstick baking mat or parchment paper. Lay the Parma ham slices flat, without overlapping. Cover with a second sheet of parchment paper and a second baking sheet. Bake the slices for approximately 15 minutes or until ham has become dehydrated and crispy. Remove to a rack to cool. The natural juices will evaporate, accentuating the salty taste.

SMOKED BACON EMULSION. Heat the whipping cream in a medium saucepan with the smoked bacon. Remove from heat and infuse for 30 minutes. Remove the bacon and reheat before serving.

Seared Sea Scallops

12 sea scallops

olive oil

fine salt

1 tablespoon salted butter

—

You can prepare the scallops beforehand and reheat gently before serving.

SEARED SEA SCALLOPS. Rinse the scallops, if needed, and dry with paper towels. Heat the olive oil in a heavy skillet to nearly smoking. Season the scallops on both sides with fine salt and place in the hot skillet. Sear one side about 1 minute. Turn using tongs and sear 1 minute on the other side. Add the butter, lower the heat, and baste for 1 minute. Remove to absorbent paper. Keep warm in a 195°F (90°) oven.

SERVE. Warm the lentils and the smoky bacon emulsion. Place some warm lentils on a small plate, top with a sea scallop. Emulsify the warm cream using a hand blender. Top the scallop with some foam and finish with a small chip of Parma ham.

—

Serves 6. Prep time: 30 minutes. Cook time: 50 minutes plus 30 minutes for infusing.

MAIN COURSE

LIGHTLY BATTERED DEEP-FRIED PRAWNS

with Tartar Sauce

---

18 prawns

Batter

3½ ounces (100 g) flour

½ ounce (15 g) baking powder

1¾ ounces (50 g) cornstarch

1 egg

about ⅓ cup (75 g) *fromage blanc,* or Greek yogurt

½ cup (125 g) water

1 quart (1 l) grapeseed, oil for frying

fleur de sel

Tartar Sauce

1 egg yolk

1 tablespoon hot mustard

about 8½ fl. ounces (250 g) grapeseed oil

1 tablespoon white balsamic vinegar

fine salt, pepper

¼ white onion, finely chopped

¼ bunch Italian parsley, minced

large pinch of capers

3 small pickles, chopped

Caper berries, for garnish

PRAWNS. Remove the heads and peel the prawns. Make a small incision in the back of the prawn using a sharp knife and remove the intestines. Keep refrigerated until ready for use.

LIGHT BATTER FOR DEEP-FRYING. Sift the flour, baking soda and cornstarch together into a medium-sized mixing bowl. Whisk in the egg, then the *fromage blanc.* The result will be a heavy paste with lots of lumps—no worries. Whisk in the water little by little until the batter becomes smooth. Refrigerate until ready for use. The batter should be used within 30 minutes. It doesn't keep well due to the baking powder.

Heat the grapeseed oil in a heavy saucepan to 350°F (180°C). Dip the prawns into the batter; remove with a slotted spoon and place gently into hot oil, three at a time. Using a wire skimmer, turn the prawns regularly to brown on all sides and remove from oil when golden. Place on absorbent paper and sprinkle with fleur de sel.

TARTAR SAUCE. Make sure all ingredients are room temperature before starting. Place the egg yolk in dry bowl. Whisk in the hot mustard and then the oil, little by little. The mayonnaise should be light in color and very creamy. Add the white balsamic vinegar, season with salt and pepper. Add the chopped onion, parsley, capers, and pickles. Check seasoning. Cover and keep chilled until ready for use.

SERVE. Place the warm, golden prawns on a serving platter, place a bowl of spicy tartar sauce in the middle, and add a few caper berries. Make sure you grab one for yourself; they will disappear in a flash!

Serves 6. Prep time: 40 minutes. Cook time: 8 minutes.

MAIN COURSE

BEEF CUBES MARINATED IN SWEET SAKE AND MISO

with Butternut Squash Discs in Grapefruit and Orange Reduction with Ginger

1 butternut squash

⅔ tablespoon (10 g) fresh ginger

3 pink grapefruits

2 oranges

1 cup (25 cl) mirin (sweet sake for cooking)

5 fl. ounces (15 cl) rice vinegar

1 tablespoon dark miso paste

About 1½ pounds (600 g) beef *onglet*, or hangar steak

2 tablespoons sesame oil

1 tablespoon olive oil

edible pansy flowers

—

Tips from a Pro

Marinate the beef cubes overnight; the rice vinegar will slightly cook the meat and will only need to be seared before serving.

Slice the ends off the butternut squash and peel using a sharp knife. Cut in thin slices. Using a round cookie cutter, cut out perfect discs.

Peel and slice the ginger. Juice 2 of the grapefruits and the oranges. Pour the juices into a sauté pan, add the sliced ginger, and place the discs of squash in the juice without overlapping. Heat the squash discs at medium heat then reduce to low until the juices have evaporated. Squash should be slightly candied and tender. If necessary, add some water to finish the cooking. Do not overcook; the discs need to be firm enough to be held in the hand. Peel the last grapefruit using a paring knife to remove the pith. Supreme the grapefruit (remove the wedges by cutting on either side of the white membrane) and hold over a small bowl to collect the juice. Pour the grapefruit juice over the cooked squash discs. Set the grapefruits sections aside.

In a small bowl, mix the mirin with the rice vinegar. Add the miso paste and whisk.

Cut the beef into bite-sized pieces and place into a shallow dish and pour in the marinade. Marinate for 45 minutes.

Heat the two oils in a heavy frying pan. Remove beef from marinade and dry slightly on absorbent paper. No need to salt the meat before cooking; the miso paste is already quite salty. Sear the meat on both sides in the hot oil. Cook for 2 to 3 minutes, lower the heat slightly, and add the marinade. Reduce to a syrup consistency. Using a pastry brush, coat the meat with the marinade.

SERVE. Arrange the butternut squash discs on a serving platter. Place a piece of warm, well-coated beef in the center, add a grapefruit section, and top with an edible pansy flower.

—

Serves 6 (3 bites per person). Prep time: 30 minutes. Marinade: 45 minutes. Cook time: 25 minutes.

MAIN COURSE

FREE-RANGE CHICKEN BREAST BITES

with Coconut, Turmeric, and Kaffir Lime Grilled on an Open Fire

4 free-range chicken
breasts

1 quart (1 l) coconut milk

2 teaspoons nuoc man
sauce

¼ ounce (6 g) ground
turmeric

zest of 2 kaffir limes

3 kaffir leaves

Slice the chicken breasts in long strips. Mix the coconut milk, nuoc man, turmeric, kaffir lime zest, and lime leaves, making a very flavorful marinade. Place chicken strips in a shallow dish and cover with marinade. Cover in plastic wrap and refrigerate for 40 minutes.

Thread the chicken strips onto metal or bamboo skewers. Grill over an open fire for approximately 8 to 10 minutes until golden and fully cooked inside. The metal skewers can get very hot; watch out for burns. The skewers may also be grilled inside on a well-oiled grill pan for the same amount of time.

SERVE. Place warm on a large platter. Season by brushing some of the marinade over the top then zest a kaffir lime using a microplane.

—

Makes 12 skewers. Prep time: 20 minutes. Cook time: 8 minutes.

CHEESE

ROQUEFORT AND PEAR PUFFS

8.8 ounces (250 g) puff
pastry

½ cup (120 g) Roquefort
cheese

3 pears

juice of 1 lemon

black pepper

Preheat oven to 390°F (200°C). Roll out the puff pastry. Cut out 1-inch x
3-inch (3 cm x 9 cm) rectangles. Place them on a baking sheet covered with
a nonstick baking mat. Cover with a sheet of parchment paper and place
another baking sheet over the top. Bake for 25 minutes until golden brown
and fully cooked through. Baking the puff pastry between 2 baking sheets
keeps it from rising too much, making it very light and crispy. Remove to
rack to cool.

Cut thin slices of Roquefort and peel and slice the pears in thin quarters.
Squeeze lemon juice over the pears to keep them from oxidizing.

Just before serving, place a slice of Roquefort and a slice or two of pear
on the puff pastry rectangles. Arrange on a baking sheet and heat in oven
for 5 minutes until Roquefort is melted and slightly golden. Ground some
fresh black pepper over the top. Serve warm. These, too, will disappear very
quickly!

—

Makes 12 puffs. Prep time: 25 minutes. Cook time: 35 minutes.

DESSERT

INDIVIDUAL-SIZED FRESH FRUIT CRUMBLE

with Toasted Walnuts

Variant 1

2 pears

3 red plums

about ¾ cup (200 g) red
currants

2 tablespoons salted
butter

3 tablespoons muscovado
sugar

12 toasted walnuts,
slightly chopped

2 teaspoons ground
ginger

Variant 2

2 apples

4 green plums

2 tablespoon salted butter

3 tablespoons muscovado
sugar

2 teaspoons Ceylon
cinnamon

12 toasted walnuts,
slightly chopped

Crumble

7 ounces (200 g) salted
butter, room temperature

7 ounces (200 g) brown
sugar

7 ounces (200 g) flour

3½ ounces (100 g)
organic oatmeal flakes

FRUIT. Wash, peel, and cut all fruit into small cubes. In two separate
sauté pans, melt the butter until foamy in each, and then add the sugar
and caramelize for 2 minutes. Add the pears and red plums in one, and
apples and green plums in the other, and walnuts and spices. Stew over
medium heat just until the fruit renders its natural juice, approximately
10 to 15 minutes. Remove to separate bowls.

CRUMBLE. Preheat oven to 350°F (180°C). In a medium-sized mixing
bowl, mix the butter with the sugar using your clean fingertips. Add the
flour, continue mixing, and then add the oatmeal.

Cover a baking sheet with a nonstick baking mat, and form small hazel-
nut-sized balls of crumble batter. Place the balls of batter on the baking
sheet and bake for 20 to 25 minutes until golden and crunchy.

Fill 12 individual ramekins with the different fruit and walnut compote.
Cover with the golden crumble and bake for approximately 5 minutes
until just warmed. Serve.

—

Serves 12. Prep time: 40 minutes. Cook time: 45 minutes.

DESSERT

EXTRA-MOIST CHOCOLATE CAKE WITH A CARAMEL CENTER

Salted Butter Caramel

5.3 ounces (150 g) sugar

5 fl. ounces (150 g) heavy whipping cream

6.3 ounces (180 g) salted butter, cut in cubes

Cake

2 eggs

1¾ ounces (50 g) sugar

1 ounce (30 g) flour

3½ ounces (100 g) butter

3½ ounces (100 g) good dark chocolate

CARAMEL. Pour half of the sugar in a medium saucepan. Heat over medium until sugar melts, add the rest of the sugar, and continue heating until fully melted and browned to a golden amber color. Do not stir the sugar while it's melting; the utensil will cool down the sugar and it will mass, making a hard block of sugar. Remove caramel from heat. Heat the whipping cream and pour onto the caramel. Careful—the cream will be cooler than the caramel and it will spatter a bit. Put back onto medium heat and mix well using a spatula. The cream should be fully blended and the temperature should decrease to 226°F (108°C). Remove caramel from heat and whisk in the cubes of butter little by little. Let cool in refrigerator for 15 minutes.

Form the caramel into balls by rolling in the palms of your clean hands. Set aside.

CHOCOLATE CAKE. Preheat oven to 350°F (180°C). In a medium mixing bowl, whisk the eggs and sugar until frothy and lightened in color. Add the flour and whisk just to mix the flour. Melt the chocolate and butter together over a water bath. Let the chocolate cool slightly and add to the egg mixture. Whisk lightly.

Pour the chocolate batter into small silicone molds about ¾ of the way. Add the caramel center and refrigerate for 1 hour. The batter may be made 2 days in advance and chilled in the molds.

Place silicone molds onto a baking sheet and bake at 350°F (180°C) for 10 to 12 minutes. Let cool a bit before unmolding. Arrange onto a pretty serving dish, and cut a few open in the middle to show the flowing caramel. Oh so yummy!

—

Makes 12 small portions. Prep time: 40 minutes. Cook time: 20 minutes.

DESSERT

PRALINE AND CHOCOLATE NIB *FINANCIERS*

11½ fl. ounces (340 g) butter

9.2 ounces (260 g) powdered sugar

2.8 ounces (80 g) almond powder

5.3 ounces (150 g) hazelnut powder

3½ ounces (100 g) flour

8 (240 g) egg whites

1½ ounces (40 g) pralines, crushed

1 ounce (30 g) chocolate nibs

Melt the butter and continue heating until the butter becomes a hazelnut color *(beurre noisette)*. Strain the butter through a fine sieve. In a large mixing bowl, whisk the powdered sugar, the almond and hazelnut powders, and the flour.

Using a spatula, add the egg whites and mix well. Then add the melted butter by mixing gently with the spatula. Pour the batter into a pastry bag and refrigerate for 1 hour. This batter may be made several days in advance and freezes well.

Preheat oven to 390°F (200° C). Fill silicone *financiers* molds using the pastry bag. Sprinkle half with crushed pralines and the other half with chocolate nibs. Bake the *financiers* for 6 to 8 minutes. Remove to rack to cool.

—

Makes 40 mini financiers. *Prep time: 30 minutes. Cook time: 8 minutes.*

DESSERT

MINI *MONT BLANC* CAKES

Cream

1.4 ounces (40 g) butter, softened

5.3 ounces (150 g) chestnut purée, room temperature

1 teaspoon dark rum

6¾ fl. ounces (200 g) heavy whipping cream

Dough

4.4 ounces (125 g) butter, room temperature

1.6 ounces (45 g) powdered sugar

salt

4 ounces (115 g) flour

CREAM. In a mixer with the whisk attachment, whisk the soft butter until light and creamy. Add the chestnut purée by thirds and whisk rapidly. The chestnut purée must be room temperature. If cold, it will harden the butter and will not mix to a creamy texture. Add the rum and continue mixing. Fill a pastry bag fitted with a small tip.

Place the mixing bowl and the heavy whipping cream in the freezer for 15 minutes. Start whipping slowly at first, increasing the speed little by little. When the cream holds in the whisk and makes firm peaks, stop whipping. Fill a second pastry bag fitted with a small round tip and refrigerate until ready for use.

DOUGH. Preheat oven to 340°F (170°C). Using a mixer with the paddle attachment, mix the soft butter with the powdered sugar to obtain a creamy the texture. Add about 1 gram of salt and continue mixing. Add the flour and mix vigorously. Roll the soft dough between two sheets of parchment paper, about ¼- inch thick. The amount of butter in this recipe will make the dough crunchy and delicious, however, it will also make it quite fragile. Refrigerate for 30 minutes, as the cold dough will be much easier to work with.

Using a small, square cookie cutter, cut out perfect squares and place on a baking sheet covered with a nonstick baking mat. Bake 10 to 12 minutes until slightly browned. Remove to a rack to cool.

SERVE. Using the pastry bag with the whipping cream, pipe out the cream, forming a dome shape on each butter cookie. Place the cookies with the cream on a rack and partially cover with chestnut purée cream by using a back and forth motion. Remove to a serving platter and sprinkle with powdered sugar. Keep refrigerated until serving. The *mont blanc* are best when fresh. You'll need to serve and eat them right away, but believe me, that won't be tough to do!

Makes 24 portions. Prep time: 40 minutes. Cook time: 12 minutes.

MENU 09

MY STAR RESTAURANT DINNERS—FRESH FROM THE SEA

Appetizer

Wild Atlantic Mackerel in a Chardonnay-Fennel
Marinade with Crispy Mackerel Skin Chips

Meagre Carpaccio with Fresh Lime Vinaigrette
and Salicornia Emulsion

Main Course

Tiger Prawns from Madagascar and Roasted
Squash Gnocchi with Verbena Prawn Emulsion
and Roasted Shiitake

Dessert

French Vanilla Ice Cream Macarons with Fresh
Mangoes

S ometimes you just really want to make a very special meal, regardless of the time needed in preparation. Delicious, of course, but also perfectly executed. One of those dinners where you can see the "wow" in the eyes of each guest as you serve dish after dish. One of those meals where you get that tickle of self-satisfaction when you see what you've achieved, making it all worthwhile.

My star restaurant menus are that kind of meal. Working as a professional chef over the years has taught me endless techniques and tricks, many of which can be used right in your home kitchen. You will find several within each recipe.

How you plate your dishes will make all the difference. Your menu will go from cozy, family-style to star-restaurant appeal by designing the aesthetics of your plate. A few hints:

• First, think in advance how the dish should be plated; a few sketches will help. This will prevent mishaps while your guests are patiently waiting for their gourmet meal.

• Use white plates, the food is the star.

• Place the main feature of the dish first, and then add the accompaniments, condiments, emulsions, and sauces. Never put the sauce directly on the main element, it should be served on the side in a small sauce dish.

• Finish with beautiful, fresh herbs, sprouts, or flowers. Everything on the plate must be edible and enhance the taste of the main dish.

• Plate elements in odd numbers—3, 5, or 7 pieces—are more visually balanced then 2, 4, or 6.

• Be sure to leave space on the plate. A plate that is too full may be comforting but is never very appetizing.

• And lastly, prepare small pieces of paper towel to quickly wipe up drips and spills before presenting the plates.

WILD ATLANTIC MACKEREL IN A CHARDONNAY-FENNEL MARINADE

with Crispy Mackerel Skin Chips

Mackerel

4 very fresh wild Atlantic mackerels

Marinade

2 young carrots

1 sweet white onion

1 bulb fennel

1 organic lemon

about 5 fl. ounces (150) g olive oil

4 sprigs fresh thyme

1 bay leaf

10 black pepper corns

2½ fl. ounces (75 g) Xeres vinegar

⅘ cup (20 cl) chardonnay

⅘ cup (20 cl) water

10 black peppercorns

MACKEREL. Filet the mackerels using a sharp, thin bladed knife. Mackerels are easy to filet because the skin has no scales and the flesh is quite soft. Delicately remove the stomach portion of the filet by cutting at a slant. It's always a bit fatty and not nice on the plate. Cover in plastic wrap and refrigerate.

MACKEREL SKIN CHIPS. Preheat oven to 350°F (180°). Remove the skin using the same sharp knife. Lay the filet before you on a cutting board skin-side down. Slide the knife between the skin and the flesh starting at the tail. Slide the knife gently back and forth, keeping the blade perfectly flat and parallel to the cutting board. Hold the skin by the tail to keep it from rolling up as you remove it.

Cover a baking tray with parchment paper. Lay the mackerel skin perfectly flat on the parchment paper, cover with a second sheet of parchment, and a second baking sheet. Bake for approximately 20 minutes. The natural oils in the skin will slightly fry and make it crispy. Remove to a rack to cool.

MARINADE. Peel and wash the carrots, slice thinly. Peel the sweet onion and slice thinly. Cut off the tips of the fennel, slice in two lengthwise. Remove the core using a paring knife and thinly slice each fennel half. Wash the lemon and slice thinly as well.

In a large pot, heat 3 tablespoons of olive oil. Add the sprigs of thyme and the bay leaf, and heat gently. Add the sliced vegetables and the slices of lemon. Sweat 2 to 3 minutes, adding a bit more olive oil if necessary. Add the vinegar and chardonnay, bring to a boil, and let the alcohol evaporate. Add the rest of the olive oil, water, and the peppercorns. Simmer for 10 minutes then remove from heat.

Place the chilled mackerel filets on a cutting board and slice 1-inch pieces at an angle to form a diamond shape. Place the mackerel slices skin-side down in a shallow dish. Pour the warm marinade over the top to just cover the slices. Cover in plastic wrap and cool in refrigerator overnight. The vinegar and lemon will slightly cook the filets.

The next day, remove the filets to absorbent paper. Filter the marinade, separating the vegetables from the liquid.

SERVE. On a small plate, place a nice mackerel skin chip then a piece of marinated filet. Add some fennel, onion, and lemon, then season with a spoon of marinade. Serve with dry white wine, Champagne brut, or Prosecco.

—

Serves 4. Prep time: 30 minutes. Cooking time: 30 minutes.

APPETIZER

MEAGRE CARPACCIO

with Fresh Lime Vinaigrette and Salicornia Emulsion

Carpaccio

1 fresh meagre,
approximately (2¼
pounds, 1 kg)

Salicornia Emulsion

about ⅔ cup (150 g) fresh
Salicornia

10 fl. ounces (300 g)
heavy whipping cream

Lime Vinaigrette

2 fresh limes

fleur de sel

olive oil

small leaves Thai basil

Maigre, or meager in English, is often confused with sea bass. The flesh of the maigre is white and firm and very light in taste. It is a wonderful fish to use in season but could be replaced by any other white-fleshed, mild local fish.

The delicious Salicornia used in the recipe doesn't really have an accurate translation. It is a sweet and salty weed that grows near salt marches. It doesn't actually grow in the sea but needs to be near sea water.

CARPACCIO. Scale and filet the fish. Remove the stomach portion. Place the filets in the freezer for 10 minutes to firm the flesh. Select the round plates you'll be using to plate the dish. Trace a perfect circle using a pencil onto a small, square sheet of parchment paper; the circle should be half the size of the plate.

Remove the filets from the freezer. Using a sharp knife, cut thin strips off the filets by sliding the knife from the tail toward the head in the direction of the flesh. Turn the traced parchment paper over (you don't want the pencil marks to transfer to the fish!) and place the thin strips of meagre delicately onto the circle pattern without overlapping. Smooth out the edges of the circle using a paring knife.

Cover the fish with a second square of parchment paper and refrigerate until ready for use.

SALICORNIA EMULSION. Rinse the Salicornia. Chop roughly and place into a medium-sized saucepan with the whipping cream. Bring to a boil, reduce heat, and simmer for 10 to 12 minutes. Mix well using an immersion blender. Strain through a fine sieve and pour into a clean, small saucepan.

VINAIGRETTE. Zest one lime and juice two. Whisk the lime juice with the zest, fleur de sel, and then olive oil.

PLATING. Remove the carpaccio from the refrigerator. Remove the top piece of parchment and turn the other sheet over onto the plate delicately. The circle should be off-center. Once placed, gently remove the last sheet of parchment.

Using a brush, lightly cover the carpaccio with the lime vinaigrette and place a few leaves of Thai basil.

Heat the Salicornia emulsion and mix with an immersion blender to create a nice froth. Place 1 tablespoon of the emulsion on the plate and decorate with a sprig of Salicornia. Add some fleur de sel and freshly zested lime.

—

Serves 4. Prep time: 30 minutes. Cook time: 5 minutes.

MAIN COURSE

TIGER PRAWNS FROM MADAGASCAR AND ROASTED SQUASH GNOCCHI

with Verbena Prawn Emulsion and Roasted Shiitake

Prawns

12 tiger prawns

olive oil

Mushrooms

3¼ pounds (1,5 kg) shiitake mushrooms

salted butter

olive oil

salt, pepper

Gnocchi

½ pound (250 g) buttercup squash

sea salt

½ pound (250 g) potatoes with starch

about 1 cup (250 g) flour

1 egg

salt, pepper

nutmeg

cornstarch

PRAWNS. Remove the heads, peel the prawns, and set aside for the sauce. Make a small incision in the back of the prawn using a sharp knife and remove the intestine.

Keep refrigerated until ready for use.

MUSHROOMS. Rinse rapidly in cool water and place immediately onto a clean towel to dry. Never leave the shiitake in the water; they are like mushroom sponges! Slice in two or four depending on size and set aside.

GNOCCHI. Rinse the buttercup squash and slice in two. Remove the seeds using a large spoon. Slice into large quarters. Cover the bottom of a baking dish with coarse sea salt, add the quarters of squash and the potatoes (skin on), and bake in a 350°F (180°C) oven for 20 to 25 minutes until flesh is tender. Baking in the oven will develop the natural sugars in both the squash and potatoes, and it will also dry out the flesh a bit, making the gnocchi dough much easier to work with.

When finished baking, peel the potatoes and the squash and scoop out the flesh.

Pass the potatoes through a food mill then through a drum sieve. Mix the squash using an immersion blender, and pass through a sieve if the squash is still a bit wet. Mix the two together. Let cool before adding the next ingredients.

Using your clean hands, add the flour then the egg, salt, pepper, and freshly grated nutmeg. Divide the dough into 4 long rolls, about ¾ inches thick. Cut ¾ –inch-long pieces. Using the back of a fork, roll the gnocchi along the tines, making an imprint. The grooves will catch the sauce.

Place the gnocchi on a tray and sprinkle with cornstarch to keep them from being damp. Place in refrigerator until ready to use. The gnocchi may be made the day before and kept refrigerated.

Prawn Emulsion

1 sweet white onion

1 carrot

2 tomatoes

1 stalk celery

4–5 tablespoons olive oil

heads and shells of prawns

8 fresh verbena leaves

⅔ cup (15 cl) dry white wine

1 quart (1 l) heavy whipping cream

2 tablespoons tomato concentrate

1 tablespoon butter, warm

4 tablespoons olive oil

salt, pepper

PRAWN EMULSION. Peel and dice the sweet onion. Peel and slice the carrot. Slice tomatoes into quarters, and wash and slice the celery stalk. Heat the olive oil in a large saucepan. Add the heads and shells of the prawns. Add some of the verbena leaves, and sweat over medium heat. The shells will turn red as you heat them. Add the vegetables, stir, and sweat for 5 to 6 minutes on medium heat. Increase the heat and deglaze with the white wine. Let the alcohol evaporate. Add the heavy whipping cream and the tomato concentrate. Bring to a boil, reduce heat, add the remaining verbena leaves, and simmer for 50 to 60 minutes on low heat. The cream will reduce to about half and the flavors will concentrate. Strain the emulsion through a fine sieve and keep warm in a medium saucepan.

FINAL PREP. Boil a large pot with salted water. Drop in the gnocchi. When they rise to the surface, they're ready. Strain and keep warm in a nonstick pan with 1 tablespoon of frothy salted butter.

Heat 2 tablespoons olive oil in a heavy skillet. Toss in the quartered mushrooms and sauté over high heat until they lose their natural liquid. Lower heat, add a tablespoon of salted butter, and continue sautéing until the mushrooms become slightly roasted. Season with salt and pepper.

Heat 2 more tablespoons olive oil in a nonstick pan. Season the prawns with salt and pepper. Sear on both sides over medium heat approximately 3 to 4 minutes total. The prawns should not be overcooked. Remove to absorbent paper.

PLATING. Line up 3 gnocchi on the left-hand side of the plate. Place a warm, roasted prawn over the top of each. Using an immersion blender, blend the hot prawn emulsion until frothy. Spoon the emulsion generously over the prawns and gnocchi. Add the warm shiitake mushrooms and finish with fresh verbena leaves. Serve warm.

Serves 4. Prep time: 45 minutes. Cooking time: 1 hour and 40 minutes.

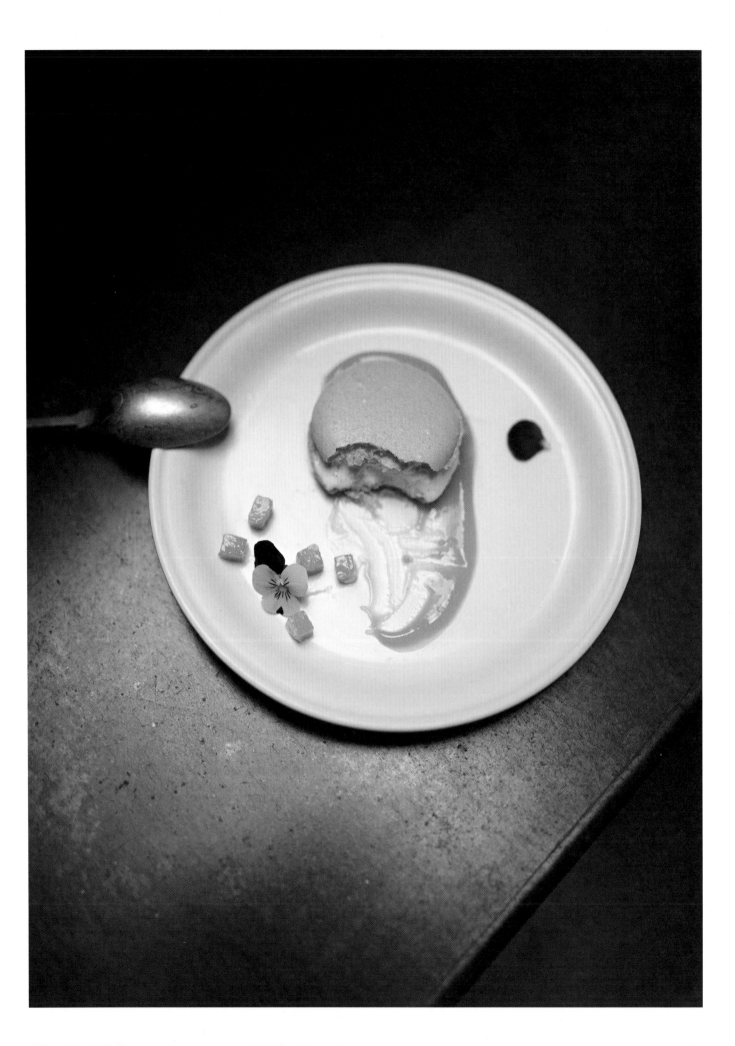

DESSERT

FRENCH VANILLA ICE CREAM MACARONS WITH FRESH MANGOES

Macaron

3½ ounces (100 g) almond meal

3½ ounces (100 g) powdered sugar

about 3 fl. ounces (90 g) egg white

3½ ounces (100 g) sugar

Orange food coloring

Ice Cream

for ¾ of a quart

1 vanilla bean

1¼ cups (300 g) whole milk

6¾ fl. ounces (200 g) heavy whipping cream

4 egg yolks

3¼ ounces (90 g) sugar

Mangoes

2 ripe mangoes

edible pansy flower

About egg whites: For best results, separate the whites from the yolks 3 days in advance. Keep the whites in an airtight container in the refrigerator. Use the yolks immediately, for a pastry cream or mayonnaise, for example. If you don't use them right away, discard them. The yolks cannot be kept.

MACARONS. Preheat oven to 300°F (150°C). Place the almond meal and the powdered sugar together in the food processor. Pulse several times until you obtain a well-mixed powder. Do not over pulse; you don't want the natural oil in the almond meal to come to the surface. Sift the powder through a drum sieve to make sure it is perfectly mixed. Place into a large mixing bowl.

Beat the egg whites, adding the sugar little by little until you have a soft-peaked meringue. Add a few drops of food coloring to the meringue and beat gently to the desired color. The macaroon shells may be colorful, but I don't flavor them. Traditionally, they should have that wonderful almond taste.

Add a large spatula full of meringue to the powder mixture. Mix well at first. You should have a pasty texture. Add the meringue, in three parts, mixing gently each time. Use a large rubber spatula for this—never a whisk. Always turn your spatula in the same direction, from bottom to top to mix; this will keep you from overmixing. The "macaronade" should be smooth, semi thick, and shiny. When you lift some batter up with your spatula, it should fall back into the bowl in ribbon fashion. Fill a pastry bag fitted with a small (approximately 10mm) round tip.

Prepare baking sheets with parchment paper. Place a dot of batter in each of the four corners to "glue" the parchment paper to the baking sheet. This will keep it from blowing about in the convection oven. Pipe out even-sized dollops of batter in straight lines. Be sure to leave space between them; they will expand. Tap the baking sheet on the edge of the counter to flatten the dollops and remove any air bubbles. Let the dollops of batter air-dry for approximately 15 minutes. The surface should no longer be sticky when touched with the tip of your finger. Bake the macarons for 12 to 14 minutes. Remove from oven and slide the parchment paper to a rack to cool.

ICE CREAM. Scrape the seeds from the vanilla pod using the tip of a sharp knife. Heat the milk, cream, and the vanilla seeds to just before boiling in a medium saucepan. In a medium mixing bowl, whisk the egg yolks and sugar until the yolks become frothy and lighten in color. Pour the hot milk/cream over the egg yolks, whisk, and pour back into the saucepan. Heat to just before boiling; the mixture will thicken slightly and should coat the spoon. Pour into a clean mixing bowl and cool. Pour the mixture into the ice cream maker and churn until creamy. Keep in freezer until ready to serve. Homemade ice cream will always be creamier than the store-bought version.

Arrange the macarons by pairs. Fill a piping bag with the vanilla ice cream and place a good dollop on one of the macaron shells. Cover with the second and keep in the freezer until ready to serve.

MANGOES. Remove the skin from the mangoes using a sharp paring knife. Cut thick slices of one mango; slice into sticks and then into evenly sized cubes. With the second, remove the ripe flesh, cutting around the pit, and mix using an immersion blender to make a semi-thick purée.

PLATING. Using a pastry brush dipped in the mango purée, paint a nice stripe of mango in the center of a round plate. Place the cold macaron in the center. Decorate with an uneven number of mango cubes and an edible pansy flower, if available.

—

Makes 12 macaroons. Prep Time: 30 minutes. Cook time: 33 minutes.

MENU 10

MY STAR RESTAURANT
DINNERS — MEAT

Appetizer
Portobello Mushroom Tart with Sweet Onion
Compote and Pancetta

Semi-Cooked Duck Foie Gras with Candied
Citrus

Main Course
Lamb Tenderloin Roasted in Salted Butter,
Artichoke Purée and Baby Artichokes *Barigoule*
Style, with Lamb Jus and Artichoke Reduction

Dessert
Double Chocolate Whipped Ganache Tart

I so love this menu.

It features the type of dishes that are normally ordered in only a fine, French restaurant. Actually making them in your own kitchen seems, to say the least, a bit intimidating, but not to worry! Yes, this menu does require some work, but since when does reward come without effort?

Michelin star dishes like foie gras, lamb tenderloin, artichokes, lamb demi glace, and whipped ganache are included in this special meal—and they are all fully achievable at home.

Start by carefully reading each recipe. Make a good shopping list and take a few notes on how to get organized. Be thoughtful about your guest list as well: five gourmet friends and yourself at the table sounds like a good start to me.

Next step, slip on your favorite apron and your chef shoes, and you're on your way to culinary bliss!

PORTOBELLO MUSHROOM TART

with Sweet Onion Compote and Pancetta

1 round puff pastry, all butter

3 sweet, white onions

3 tablespoons salted butter

salt, pepper

6 to 8 small, firm portobello mushrooms

4 tablespoons duck fat

6 thin slices of Italian pancetta

Fresh beet greens

Preheat oven to 395°F (200°C). Using a 4-inch (10-cm) round cookie cutter, cut out 6 perfect circles from the puff pastry. Place on a baking sheet covered in parchment paper and chill in refrigerator.

Peel and thinly slice the sweet onions. Warm the salted butter in a heavy, nonstick skillet until frothy and sweat the sweet onions on medium heat. Mix gently, lightly coating in the salted butter. Season the onions with salt and pepper and continue cooking slowly until onions have fully melted, about 15 minutes; they should remain white in color and sweet in taste. Once cooked, set aside on a plate to cool.

Remove puff pastry rounds from refrigerator, cover in a second sheet of parchment paper and a second baking sheet, and bake for approximately 20 minutes until golden brown. Remove to a rack to cool.

Clean the stems of the portobello mushrooms using a paring knife if necessary. Brush the tops using a damp mushroom brush or simple a wet paper towel. Never plunge portobello mushrooms in water; they will absorb it all. Remove stems and save for another use. Using a sharp knife, cut the caps in thin slices.

Heat 2 tablespoons of duck fat in the same skillet used for the onions. Heat the portobello mushroom cups until slightly browned on both sides, and season with salt and pepper. Remove to absorbent paper.

Cover each puff pastry round with a thin layer of sweet onions. Arrange the portobello slices so that they slightly overlap. Cut the pancetta slices in two, twist in a corkscrew fashion, and place on top of the tartlets. Using a brush, coat lightly with the rest of the melted duck fat and bake in oven at 350°F (180°C) until pancetta is crispy and the tartlets are heated, approximately 10 minutes. Garnish with beet greens. Serve warm.

Serves 6. Prep time: 30 minutes. Cook time: 51 minutes.

APPETIZER

SEMI-COOKED DUCK FOIE GRAS

with Candied Citrus

Fois Gras

1 raw, fatted duck liver from the Landes region of France, (1 pound, or 500 g)

1 teaspoon (5 g) salt

1¼ teaspoons (2.5 g) white pepper

¼ teaspoon (0.5 g) allspice

⅛ teaspoon (0.25 g) ground cardamom

¼ teaspoon (1 g) sugar

¼ cup (5 cl) white sherry

freshly ground black pepper

black Hawaiian salt

Candied Citrus

2 organic lemons

1 organic lime

½-inch piece fresh ginger

about 3⅓ fl. ounces (100 g) cane sugar

3½ ounces (100 g) rice vinegar

How to choose a duck liver for foie gras? It should be light and evenly colored without bruises. When pressed gently, the liver should indent then come back to its original shape. You will need to prepare and poach the foie gras eight days before serving.

Remove the duck liver from refrigerator 1 hour before seasoning. Gently separate the two lobes. Using a small paring knife, remove the large vein between the two lobes. Remove any other surface veins.

Weigh all of the seasonings using a spice scale or spoon scale. The seasoning amounts are important and must be precise. Mix the seasoning together in a small bowl.

Rub the two lobes on all sides with the seasoning and place in a shallow dish. Cover with the white sherry, cover in plastic wrap, and place in refrigerator 24 hours to marinate. The next day, remove the dish from the refrigerator and leave at room temperature 30 minutes before preparing.

Reassemble the two lobes so that the liver takes its original shape. Prepare two overlapping sheets of heat resistant plastic wrap and place the liver in the center near the bottom. Roll into a 2¼-inch-diameter log shape. Tighten the ends by tying a knot. The roll should be perfectly airtight. Cover in a piece of aluminum foil.

Fill a large pot with water and heat to exactly 150°F (66°C)—you will need a thermometer. This temperature is important; it will ensure that the foie gras is cooked gently and fully through. You will need to maintain the water at this temperature throughout the cooking time. Place the foie gras log into the water and cover with a plate a bit smaller than the pot. The plate will keep the foie gras emerged in the water, instead of floating on the surface. For a semi-cooked foie gras or *mi-cuit*, count 40 minutes cooking time.

Baguette, thinly sliced
and toasted

Tips from a Pro

*When making foie gras, make
several lobes at the same time.
It is so delicious and makes
for a wonderful appetizer on
special occasions. I also love
to package it up in a beautiful
linen kitchen towel and offer it
as a gift to my good friends!*

Prepare a large bowl of water with ice. Plunge the cooked foie gras log
into the ice water to stop the cooking. Once fully chilled, approximately
15 minutes, place log in a shallow dish and refrigerate for eight days
before serving. Eight days is the ideal amount of time so that the flavors
have time to develop and the liver rests. A few days less is okay, but I do
not advise going beyond this time. If you want to keep your foie gras
longer, it would need to be sterilized.

CANDIED CITRUS. Rinse the lemons and the lime. Peel the ginger.
Cut the lemon into thin slices. Zest the lime using a microplane and
squeeze the juice. Place the lime juice, lime zest, sugar, ginger, and rice
vinegar in a pan. Heat on medium until sugar has melted and some of
the vinegar has evaporated. Place the lemon slices in the pan without
overlapping. Lower the heat and cook slowly until most of the liquid
evaporates and lemon slices have candied. Remove the slices and slightly
reduce the leftover juice.

PLATING. Remove foie gras from refrigerator 30 minutes before serving. Remove the aluminum foil and plastic wrap and gently remove the
yellow duck fat that has congealed on the surface. You can save this fat—
it's the good one—and use it to sauté potatoes for another dish. (Yum!!)

Using a sharp, thin-bladed knife dipped in warm water, cut perfect $\frac{1}{2}$
-inch slices of the foie gras. On a large white plate, using a pastry brush,
paint a large stripe of citrus reduction and place a candied lemon slice
in the center. Add one or two slices of foie gras, and season with fresh
pepper and black Hawaiian salt. Serve with thinly sliced, freshly toasted
baguette. Traditionally, foie gras in France is served with slightly sweet
toasted brioche. I like the crunch of a wonderful baguette instead. The
foie gras is so delicious, it needs no competition for taste.

*Makes 10 portions (1 pound of duck liver). Prep time: 30 minutes. Cook time: 40
minutes.*

MAIN COURSE

LAMB TENDERLOIN

Roasted in Salted Butter, Artichoke Purée and Baby Artichokes Barigoule *Style, with Lamb Jus and Artichoke Reduction*

Artichoke Purée

6 large artichokes

juice of 1 lemon

2 tablespoons olive oil

salt, pepper

⅘ cup (200 g) chicken or vegetable stock, warm

3 tablespoons salted butter, room temperature

Baby Artichokes, Barigoule style

12 baby artichokes

juice of 1 lemon

2 shallots

1 carrot

2 tomatoes

½ bunch fresh cilantro

2 lemons

olive oil

1 teaspoon coriander seeds

1 cup (25 cl) dry white wine

⅔ cup (15 cl) vegetable stock

ARTICHOKE PURÉE. Break off the stem of the artichoke. Remove approximately ¼ of the exterior leaves by hand. Peel the artichokes (turn) using a sharp paring knife. Hold the artichokes in the palm of your hand and turn the knife, held at an angle around the artichoke, removing all of the exterior leaves as you go. The term "turn" is used here because you want to keep the round shape of the artichoke by turning around it with your knife. Stop turning when you get to the heart. Cut off the top leaves and, using a small spoon, scoop out the choke. Prepare a small bowl of water with the juice of 1 lemon. Keep the artichokes hearts in the water until ready to cook to prevent them from oxidizing.

Heat the olive oil in a heavy skillet, sweat the artichoke hearts, season with salt and pepper, and add the warm stock. Simmer until tender, approximately 15 minutes.

Remove to the bowl of the food processor using a slotted spoon. Mix with the soft, salted butter to a fine purée texture. Check the seasoning. Keep warm in a small saucepan.

BABY ARTICHOKES, *BARIGOULE* STYLE. Turn the baby artichokes as you did for the larger ones. The choke will be smaller and more tender but must be removed all the same. Keep hearts in lemon water.

Peel and dice the shallots, and peel and dice the carrot to *brunoise* (small cubes). Peel the tomatoes, slice in quarters, remove the pulp and seeds, dice to *brunoise*. Wash and dry the cilantro. Rinse the lemons, cut in thin slices. Zest the second lemon.

Heat olive oil in a heavy skillet over medium heat; add the coriander seeds and sweat the shallots. Add the artichoke hearts and brown slightly on all sides. Deglaze with the white wine and heat to evaporate the alcohol. Season with salt and pepper. Add the diced carrot and tomato, the lemon zest, the cilantro leaves plus the vegetable stock, bring to a boil, lower the heat, and simmer until artichokes are tender. Remove artichokes and reduce the cooking juices to half. Set the juice aside to

Lamb Jus and Artichoke Reduction

bones from the baby lamb saddle

1 pound (500 g) lamb collar

olive oil

salted butter

⅔ cup (15 cl) dry white wine

½ carrot, diced

1 white onion, diced

1 quart (1 l) veal stock

cooking liquid from baby artichokes

Lamb

1 young lamb tenderloin, prepared by your butcher. Ask to keep the bones from the saddle.

3 tablespoons olive oil

4 tablespoons salted butter

1 peeled clove of garlic

2 sprigs of thyme

1 bay leaf

salt, pepper

be used for the lamb jus. Put the artichokes back into the pan and keep warm, adding a bit of salted butter.

LAMB JUS. Brown the lamb collar meat and the bones in olive oil in a medium saucepan, add 1 tablespoon of salted butter, and continue browning. Deglaze with the white wine, and scrape the bottom of the saucepan using a spatula to detach the juices and browned bits. Let the alcohol evaporate, approximately 2 minutes. Add the diced carrot and onion. Add a bit more butter, if necessary, to brown the vegetables. Strain the meat and vegetables to remove excess fat. Put all back into the saucepan and add the warm veal stock. Bring to a boil and then reduce heat and simmer for 40 minutes. Skim, if necessary.

Strain through a fine sieve into a small saucepan, add the cooking liquid from the *barigoule* artichokes and reduce to half. The jus will thicken lightly and should coat the spoon. Keep warm.

LAMB. Preheat oven to 320°F (160° C). Remove the lamb tenderloin from the refrigerator at least 30 minutes before roasting. Season the lamb with salt on all sides. Heat the olive oil in an oven-resistant heavy skillet. Brown the lamb tenderloin on one side, turn over using tongs, add the salted butter, the clove of garlic, the thyme and bay leaf, lower the heat, and brown on the other side by basting continually with the frothy salted butter.

Remove skillet from heat and place in preheated oven for 20 minutes. Remove from oven, cover in aluminum foil, and set the oven to 140°F (60°C). Open the oven door for 1 minute to cool the oven and place the lamb back in the oven to keep it warm.

PLATING. Warm large white plates in the same oven as the lamb for 2 minutes. Using a simple tablespoon, scoop up a spoonful of artichoke purée and let the dollop fall onto the top-right section of the plate. Using the back of the spoon, trace a straight line with the purée. Cut the baby artichokes in two, and place them graphically along the purée. Place the carrot and tomato cubes around the artichokes.

Slice the rested lamb tenderloin into ¾ -inch slices. With a small ladle, pour a little jus on the left side of the plate and, using the back of the ladle, spread out to a perfect circle. Place the lamb on top and season with salt and fresh ground pepper. Serve the artichoke purée in a dish on the side and the sauce in a sauce bowl.

Serves 6. Prep time: 60 minutes. Cooking time: 1 hour and 35 minutes.

DESSERT

DOUBLE CHOCOLATE WHIPPED GANACHE TART

Chocolate Tart

4.4 ounces (125 g) soft butter

2.6 ounces (75 g) powdered sugar

0.9 ounces (25 g) hazelnut meal

1 teaspoon (2.5 g) cinnamon

1 egg

7 ounces (200 g) flour

2 teaspoons (5 g) baking powder

2 teaspoons (5 g) cocoa powder

Dark Chocolate Whipped Ganache

1⅔ fl. ounces (50 g) heavy whipping cream

¼ ounce (6 g) honey

3½ ounces (100 g) good-quality dark chocolate

5 fl. ounces (150 g) heavy whipping cream, cold

White Chocolate Whipped Ganache

1⅔ fl. ounces (50 g) heavy whipping cream

¼ ounce (6 g) honey

3½ ounces (100 g) good-quality white chocolate

5 fl. ounces (150 g) heavy whipping cream, cold

2 ripe passion fruits

CHOCOLATE TART. Mix the soft butter, powdered sugar, hazelnut meal, and cinnamon in the mixer using the paddle attachment. Add the egg, mix. In a separate bowl, sift the flour with the baking powder and cocoa powder. Add to the egg mixture and mix well. Place the dough onto a piece of plastic wrap and flatten into a disc shape. Cover and refrigerate overnight.

Preheat oven to 320°F (160°C). The next day, roll the dough into a large rectangle, about ¼ –inch thick. Cut into 1- x 4-inch rectangles and place on a baking sheet covered in parchment paper. Bake at 320°F (160°C) for 15 to 20 minutes. Remove to a rack to cool.

WHIPPED GANACHE. The day before, heat ¼ cup of heavy whipping cream with the honey to boiling. Place the dark chocolate in a medium-sized mixing bowl. Pour the hot cream over the chocolate and let melt for a few minutes. Mix with an immersion blender to emulsion. Add the rest of the cold heavy whipping cream and blend with the immersion blender. Place in refrigerator overnight. Proceed in the same way for the white chocolate.

The next day, place the bowl of the mixer and whisks in the freezer for 15 minutes. Remove the chocolate creams from the refrigerator and whisk slowly at first, progressively increase the speed until the ganache has the texture of light whipped cream. Do not over-whip. Remove to pastry bags fitted with a small round tip for the white chocolate and a medium-sized tip for the dark chocolate.

SERVE. Pipe out small dots of white chocolate ganache and large dots of dark chocolate ganache onto the chocolate tart base. Cut the passion fruit in two and scoop out the seeds using a teaspoon. Decorate the tart with seeds and a bit of juice. Keep refrigerated until ready to serve.

Serves 6. Prep time: 45 minutes. Cook time: 12 minutes.

M E N U 1 1

FRENCH CAPE COD

Appetizer
Mini Crab Cakes

Clam Chowder with Île de Ré New Potatoes

Main Course
Blue Brittany Lobster Roll with Lobster Coral
Remoulade Sauce

Dessert
Creamy Lemon Cheesecake

The dishes for this menu were made with the freshest possible ingredients from sea to table, one could rightly say. I loved making all of them, especially because I was cooking in one of my favorite places ever: Île de Ré. Near the port city of La Rochelle, Île de Ré is such a gem. The island reminds me so much of a well-known East Coast island in the United States that I had to call this menu French Cape Cod!

Nothing too technical here, nor too time consuming; the menu is all about finding the best produce and freshest seafood you can. This, as always, will really make the difference.

What I love about this menu is its versatility. It would make for a wonderful sunset picnic on the beach or a super satisfying backyard feast. You could even go the fancy route and serve it all with a wonderful dry Champagne; it just depends on your mood. I know you and your guests will love this. Its crunchy, creamy, buttery, and lemony—how could you not?

APPETIZER

MINI CRAB CAKES

Mayonnaise

1 egg yolk

1 teaspoon strong mustard

8½ fl. ounces (250 g) grapeseed oil

juice of 1 lemon

salt, pepper

Crab

1 tablespoon coarse sea salt

sprigs of thyme

Bay leaf

handful black peppercorns

1 pound (450 g) fresh crab claw meat

2¼ (65 g) homemade mayonnaise

1 egg

1 tablespoon mustard

1 tablespoon Worcestershire sauce

½ teaspoon hot sauce

4 spring onions

20 crackers, finely crushed

3 tablespoons olive oil

salt and freshly ground black pepper

lemon wedges, for serving

HOMEMADE MAYONNAISE. Make sure all ingredients are room temperature before starting. Place the egg yolk in dry bowl. Whisk in the strong mustard then whisk in the oil, little by little. The mayonnaise should be light and very creamy. Add the lemon juice, season with salt and pepper. Check seasoning. Cover and keep chilled until ready for use.

CRAB. Boil a large pot of water with a tablespoon of coarse sea salt, thyme, and bay leaf plus a few black peppercorns. Add the crab claws, and when water begins simmering again, count 15 minutes. Remove the claws and run them under cold water to stop the cooking. Let cool then break open using a crab cracker. Remove all of the delicious crabmeat and set aside in a medium-sized mixing bowl.

In a small bowl, whisk the homemade mayonnaise with the egg, mustard, Worcestershire sauce, and hot sauce until smooth. Slice the spring onions thinly.

In another medium bowl, lightly toss the crabmeat with the spring onions and cracker crumbs. Gently fold in the mayonnaise mixture. Cover and refrigerate for at least 1 hour.

CRAB CAKES. Scoop the crab mixture into small balls and press them lightly into a disc shape. In a large skillet, heat the oil until hot. Add the crab cakes and cook over moderately high heat until deeply golden and heated through, about 3 minutes per side. Transfer the crab cakes to plates and serve with lemon wedges.

―

Serves 6. Prep time: 40 minutes. Cook time: 15 minutes.

APPETIZER

CLAM CHOWDER

with Île de Ré New Potatoes

---

24 fresh clams (*palourdes* in French)

2 tablespoons olive oil

2 cloves garlic, 1 whole, 1 minced

⅔ cup (15 cl) dry white wine

4 bacon slices

6 spring onions, chopped

3 stalks celery, sliced

1 cup (250 g) shellfish stock

10 new potatoes from Île de Ré or fingerlings, sliced in ½-inch slices, skin on

3 sprigs fresh thyme, chopped

¼ teaspoon ground black pepper

3 parsley sprigs

1 bay leaf

2¾ cups (660 g) whole milk

8½ fl. ounces (250 g) heavy whipping cream

Sourdough bread, for serving

Fresh thyme sprigs, for garnish

———

Why are Île de Ré potatoes so good?

Something about the soil and the sea air on this 17-mile long island give these young potatoes their unique nutty flavor. Their planting and harvesting is strictly controlled and they actually have an AOC (Appellation d'origine Controlée), much like wine. There are several varieties and sizes; I like the tiny new potatoes the best. If you can find them, they will make your chowder sweet and rich in flavor.

To open the clams: Rinse the clams rapidly in cold water. Dry with absorbent paper. Heat the olive oil in a heavy skillet over high, and add the peeled clove of garlic. Add the clams and mix to coat in olive oil. Add the white wine, let the alcohol evaporate, and cover. Continue heating over medium until the clams pop open, about 4 to 5 minutes. Remove the clams and reserve the cooking juice.

Cook bacon in a heavy Dutch oven over medium-high heat until crisp. Remove bacon from pan, reserving 2 teaspoons drippings in pan. Crumble bacon; set aside. Add the spring onion, celery, and minced garlic to pan; sauté 8 minutes or until tender. Add shellfish stock, sliced potatoes, thyme, pepper, parsley, and bay leaf. Bring to a boil. Cover, reduce heat, and simmer 15 minutes or until potatoes are tender.

Combine milk and heavy whipping cream, add to the pan. Continue boiling to reduce the liquid slightly. Stir in the clams, reduce the heat, and cook 5 minutes. Discard bay leaf.

Serve piping hot, with the crumbled bacon on top and fresh sourdough bread. Garnish with thyme sprigs and freshly ground pepper.

———

Serves 4. Prep time: 30 minutes. Cook time: 25 minutes.

MAIN COURSE

BLUE BRITTANY LOBSTER ROLL

with Lobster Coral Remoulade Sauce

2 blue Brittany lobsters, about 1 pound (500 g) each

Remoulade

1 egg yolk

1 teaspoon strong mustard

1 teaspoon cooked lobster coral

8½ fl. ounces (250 g) grapeseed oil

2 teaspoons white vinegar

juice of 1 lemon

salt, pepper

Lobster Roll

2 celery stalks, diced

8 fresh red radishes, thinly sliced

2 tablespoons fresh lemon juice

pinch of cayenne pepper

4 milk bread rolls

3 tablespoons unsalted butter, melted

½ head iceberg lettuce, shredded

salt, freshly ground pepper

POACHING THE LIVE LOBSTERS. To keep the lobster tails from curling up when cooked, secure the tails by sliding a metal skewer between the meat and the shell starting at the tail. Prepare a large ice-water bath. In a very large pot of boiling salted water, cook the lobsters until they turn bright red, about 10 minutes. Using tongs, plunge the lobsters into the ice-water bath for 2 minutes, then drain.

Remove the skewers. Twist off the lobster tails and claws and remove the meat. For the claws, use a cracker, and for the tail, cut open the belly using kitchen scissors. Reserve any coral; it will be bright red when cooked. Remove and discard the intestinal vein that runs the length of each lobster tail. Cut the lobster meat into small pieces and cut the claw meat in two, then transfer to a strainer set over a bowl and refrigerate until very cold, at least 1 hour.

REMOULADE SAUCE. Make sure all ingredients are room temperature before starting.

Place the egg yolk in dry bowl. Whisk in the strong mustard and 1 tablespoon of lobster coral and then whisk in the oil, little by little. The mayonnaise should be light and very creamy. Add the white vinegar and lemon juice, and season with salt and pepper. Check seasoning. Cover and keep chilled until ready for use.

In a large bowl, mix only the lobster tail meat (leave the claw meat on the side), with the mayonnaise and season with salt and pepper. Fold in the diced celery, sliced radishes, lemon juice, and cayenne pepper until well blended.

SERVE. Preheat oven to 360°F (180°C). Open the milk bread rolls in two and spread with melted butter. Toast in the oven until golden brown. Fill the rolls with shredded lettuce, fill up with the lobster salad, add the pieces of claw meat, sprinkle with lemon juice and freshly ground pepper. Serve immediately.

Makes 4 large rolls. Prep time: 40 minutes. Cook time: 10 minutes.

DESSERT

CREAMY LEMON CHEESECAKE

Crust

about 1¼ cup (300 g) speculoos biscuits

about 4¼ fl. ounces (125 g) melted butter

1 teaspoon butter for the mold

Lemon Cream

4 gelatin leaves (8 g)

3 eggs

5.3 ounces (150 g) sugar

zest and juice of 2 lemons

1½ cups (350 g) softened cream cheese

—

Tips from a Pro

The cheesecake may be made in advance and kept refrigerated for three days at the most for maximum freshness.

CRUST. Mix the speculoos biscuits in the food processor until they are sand-like. Place an 8-inch-round pastry circle (bottomless) on a baking sheet covered in parchment paper. Butter the circle.

Mix the crushed biscuits with the melted butter and press firmly into the bottom of the pastry circle. You should have approximately a ¾ -inch-thick crust. Make sure the crust is spread evenly. Place in refrigerator to firm.

LEMON CREAM. Place the gelatin in a small bowl of cold water until it softens, about 6 minutes. Separate the yolks from the whites. Whisk the egg yolks with the sugar until they lighten in color.

Zest the lemon using a microplane and squeeze the juice. Pour the juice and zest into a small saucepan. Add the yolk and sugar mixture and cook over medium heat, whisking continuously until the mixture thickens to the consistency of custard cream. It should not boil, to avoid scrambling the eggs. Squeeze the gelatin leaves to remove excess water and add to lemon cream. Whisk briskly to melt them. Let the mixture cool a bit before whisking in the cream cheese.

Whip the egg whites to soft peaks. Fold the egg whites into the lemon cream mixture gently. Pour the cream onto the cold speculoos biscuit crust and spread evenly using an offset spatula. Let the cheesecake set in the refrigerator overnight. Serve topped with fresh lemon zest along with homemade lemonade.

—

Serves 6. Prep time: 30 minutes. Cook time: 8 minutes.

M E N U 1 2

THE FRENCH CHICKEN

Appetizers
Caramelized Chicken Wings with Roquefort Cream
Dip

Free-Range Chicken Consommé with Chicken
Dumplings

Main Course
Goat Cheese, Pine Nut, and Purple Basil Stuffed
Chicken Thighs with Quince and Celery Root Purée
and Roasted Chicken Jus

Dessert
Rice Pudding with Caramelized Almonds and
Hazelnuts and Ginger Caramel Sauce

E veryone adores chicken, especially the French.

When I was in culinary school, a whole week's classes were dedicated to the subject. We learned how to cut up a raw chicken, debone, stuff, truss, roll, roast, sauté, and fricassee. The possibilities are endless.

This menu highlights all parts of the bird, from the wings as an appetizer to the thighs, my personal favorite. Be sure to use only free-range chickens. The taste and texture of the meat is no comparison to their poor, battery-raised cousins.

This is a great family menu; there really is something for everyone. The chicken wing appetizer will have them licking their fingers, and once they've tasted the stuffed thighs, dry chicken will forever be a thing of the past!

When it's time for dessert, I love serving the creamy rice pudding in a big bowl in the center of the table with several spoons and letting everyone delve in!

APPETIZER

CARAMELIZED CHICKEN WINGS

with Roquefort Cream Dip

Chicken Wings

1¾ ounces (50 g) honey

¼ cup (50 g) good soy sauce

3 tablespoons organic ketchup

juice of 1 lemon

8 free-range chicken wings

½ bunch chives

Cream Dip

about ⅔ cup (150 g) Roquefort cheese

about 2½ fl. ounces (75 g) heavy whipping cream

freshly ground pepper

Preheat oven to 395°F (200°C). Mix the honey, soy sauce, ketchup, and lemon juice in a shallow pan. Roll the chicken wings in the marinade to thoroughly coat them. Place chicken wings on a baking sheet covered in parchment paper and bake until fully caramelized, approximately 25 minutes. Turn and baste regularly during baking. Remove to a serving dish. Wrap a chive stem around each wing, for garnish.

ROQUEFORT DIP

In a small mixing bowl, crush the Roquefort using a fork. Whisk in the whipping cream, adding a bit more if necessary. The dip should be creamy and thick enough for dipping. Season the dip with freshly ground pepper.

—

Serves 4. Prep time: 20 minutes. Cook time: 25 minutes.

APPETIZER

FREE-RANGE CHICKEN CONSOMMÉ WITH CHICKEN DUMPLINGS

Consommé

1 free-range chicken
(about 2¾ pounds or
1.2 kg)

2 carrots

1 white onion

1 leek

1 stalk celery

6 black peppercorns

6 pink peppercorns

6 flat parsley stems

1 bay leaf

4 sprigs thyme

1 tablespoon coarse sea
salt

Dumplings

1 free-range chicken
breast

about 3⅓ fl. ounces (100
g) egg white

about 1⅔ fl. ounces (50 g)
heavy whipping cream

sea salt

cayenne pepper

1 small bunch chives,
finely chopped

2 spring onions, finely
sliced, for garnish

fresh parsley, for garnish

CONSOMMÉ. Remove the breasts from the chicken; they will be used for the dumplings. Place the rest of the whole chicken in a large stockpot and fill with cold water. Bring to a heavy boil and skim the foam that will rise to the top.

During this time, peel the carrots and onion. Clean the leek and celery. Dice the onion and slice the carrot, celery, and leek. Add all the vegetables to the stock pot, as well as the peppers, parsley stems, bay leaf, and thyme. Add the coarse sea salt. Lower the heat to medium and simmer for 2 hours. Skim if necessary.

Strain the stock through a fine sieve. Keep warm in a medium saucepan. Keep the chicken meat for another use, like a chicken pot pie.

DUMPLINGS. Place the chicken breast into the bowl of a food processor. Mix well, add the egg white, and continue mixing by pulsing. This will keep the chicken from heating too much.

Add the whipping cream and mix until creamy. Season with sea salt and cayenne pepper. Add the finely chopped chives. Using two tablespoons dipped in warm water, form perfect quenelles. Keep refrigerated until ready for use.

Heat some consommé in a wide pan. The liquid should be just simmering. Place the quenelles in the simmering consommé; they will float on the surface. Poach one side for approximately 10 minutes and gently turn over using a small skimmer. Poach the other side for an additional 10 minutes. Remove to absorbent paper.

SERVE. Heat the remaining consommé to just boiling. Check the seasoning. Add a quenelle to a warm soup plate and gently pour the hot consommé over the top. Finish with a little finely sliced spring onion and some fresh parsley.

———

Serves 8. Prep time: 40 minutes. Cook time: 2 hours, 20 minutes.

MAIN COURSE

GOAT CHEESE, PINE NUT, AND PURPLE BASIL STUFFED CHICKEN THIGHS

with Quince and Celery Root Purée and Roasted Chicken Jus

Chicken

Chicken

4 large free-range chicken thighs

¼ cup (50 g) goat cheese

about 2½ tablespoons (40 g) pine nuts

1 bunch purple basil

salt, pepper

2 tablespoons olive oil

½ ounce (15 g) salted butter, cubed

Chicken Jus

1 pound (500 g) chicken wings

olive oil

salted butter

⅔ cup (15 cl) dry white wine

½ carrot, diced

1 white onion, diced

1 quart (1 l) veal stock, warm

Purée

1 bulb celeriac

2 large quinces

1 lemon

1¾ (50 g) salted butter

1 cup (250 g) vegetable or chicken stock, warm

salt, pepper

Cilantro shoots, for garnish

FOR THE CHICKEN

Preheat oven to 390°F (200°C). Using a paring knife, remove the two bones from the thigh; be careful not to damage the chicken's skin. Remove the long white tendons near the drumstick. Place the thighs skin-side down on a plate and refrigerate until ready for use.

Cut the goat cheese into small cubes. Toast the pine nuts in a small frying pan without adding any oils. Remove pine nuts when golden. Wash the basil and chop finely. Mix cheese, nuts, and basil together in a small mixing bowl.

Season the meat side of each thigh with salt and pepper. Add a heaping tablespoon of stuffing to the center of each thigh and fold the skin side up around the stuffing, making a small pouch. Place into a baking dish rounded side up. The slightly open ends will weld together while baking. Drizzle with olive oil, and add the cubes of butter on top of each thigh. Season with salt. Bake for 50 minutes. Remove from oven and cover in aluminum foil.

CHICKEN JUS. Brown the chicken wings in olive oil in a medium saucepan, add 1 tablespoon of salted butter, and continue browning. Deglaze with the white wine, scraping the bottom of the saucepan using a spatula to detach the juices and browned bits. Let the alcohol evaporate, approximately 2 minutes. Add the diced carrot and onion. Add a bit more butter if necessary to brown the vegetables. Strain the meat and vegetables to remove excess fat. Put all back into the saucepan and add the warm veal stock. Bring to a boil then reduce heat and simmer for 40 minutes. Skim, if necessary.

Strain through a fine sieve into a small saucepan and reduce to half. The jus will thicken slightly and should cover the spoon. Keep warm.

Tips from a Pro

The chicken legs for the main dishes can be filled on the day before and then stored in the refrigerator. The roast chicken will absorb the flavors of goat cheese and basil and taste even more delicious.

CELERIAC AND QUINCE PURÉE. Peel the celeriac using a sharp paring knife, then peel the quince. Rub the quinces with some lemon to keep them from oxidizing.

Cut all onto large cubes. Heat ½ ounce (15 g) of salted butter until foamy in a two medium-sized saucepans. Add the celeriac cubes to one and the quince to the other. Sweat for 5 minutes, mixing gently to coat in the salted butter. Add the warm stock, bring to a boil. Reduce the heat and cook until tender, approximately 30 minutes. The flesh of quinces is very firm and takes a while to become tender. The celeriac will become soft much faster. Strain the vegetables when tender and reserve the cooking liquid. Add the rest of the salted butter and a little cooking liquid, if necessary. Mix each using an immersion blender until creamy. Check the seasoning and keep warm.

PLATING. Slice the stuffed thighs into 4 pieces. Add a swoosh of celeriac purée on one side, the quince on the other, and some warm chicken jus. Finish with cilantro shoots.

———

4 servings. Prep time: 45 minutes. Cook time: 2 hours and 10 minutes.

DESSERT

RICE PUDDING

with Caramelized Almonds and Hazelnuts and Ginger Caramel Sauce

Rice Pudding

about ¾ cup (180g) round rice

1 quart (1 l) whole milk

1 vanilla pod

3½ ounces (100 g) sugar

Ginger Caramel Sauce

5.3 ounces (150 g) sugar

2 teaspoons fresh ginger, chopped

5 fl. ounces (150 g) heavy whipping cream

6.3 ounces (180 g) butter, cut in cubes

For the Caramelized Nuts

5.3 ounces (150 g) sugar

3 tablespoons water

about ¼ cup (50 g) fresh hazelnuts, peeled

Whipped Cream

about 10 fl. ounces (300 g) heavy whipping cream

RICE PUDDING. Bring a large saucepan of water to boil, add the round rice and blanch for 3 minutes. Strain the rice. Bring the milk to a boil with the seeds of the vanilla pod. Add the rice adjust to low heat. Simmer for 25 minutes. Add the sugar and continue cooking for 5 minutes. Remove to a dish and let cool.

GINGER CARAMEL SAUCE. Pour half the sugar in a medium saucepan. Heat at medium heat until sugar melts. Add the rest of the sugar and the ginger and continue heating until fully melted and browned to a golden amber color. Do not stir the sugar while its melting; the utensil will cool the sugar and it will mass, making a hard, block of sugar. Remove caramel from heat. Heat the whipping cream and pour onto the caramel. Careful—the cream will be cooler than the caramel and it will spatter it bit. Put back onto medium heat and mix well using a spatula. The cream should be fully blended and the temperature should go down to 226°F (108°). Remove caramel from heat and whisk in the cubes of butter little by little. Let cool to room temperature.

CARAMELIZED NUTS. Add the sugar and water to a small saucepan. Heat to 250°F (121°C). Add the peeled hazelnuts and coat with the sugar. The sugar will crystalize and turn white. Continue heating on medium heat until sugar melts again and caramelizes. Pour the hazelnuts onto a nonstick baking mat and let cool.

WHIPPED CREAM. Place the mixing bowl, the whisk, and the heavy whipping cream in the freezer for 15 minutes. Start whipping slowly at first, increasing the speed little by little. When the cream holds in the whisk and makes firm peaks, stop whipping. Fold the whipped cream gently into the cold rice pudding.

SERVE. Serve with the caramelized hazelnuts and caramel sauce drizzled on top. I like to serve this dessert in a big bowl in the middle of the table with lots of spoons!

—

Serves 6. Prep time: 20 minutes. Cook time: 20 minutes.

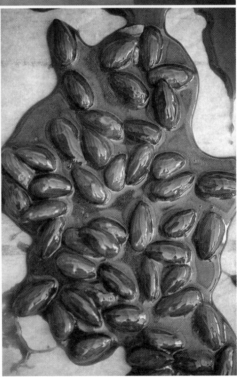

INDEX

CONVERSION CHARTS

METRIC AND IMPERIAL CONVERSIONS

(These conversions are rounded for convenience)

Ingredient	Cups/Table-spoons/ Teaspoons	Ounces	Grams/ Milliliters
Butter	1 cup = 16 tablespoons = 2 sticks	8 ounces	230 grams
Cheese, shredded	1 cup	4 ounces	110 grams
Cream cheese	1 tablespoon	0.5 ounce	14.5 grams
Cornstarch	1 tablespoon	0.3 ounce	8 grams
Flour, all-purpose	1 cup/1 tablespoon	4.5 ounces/0.3 ounce	125 grams/8 grams
Flour, whole wheat	1 cup	4 ounces	120 grams
Fruit, dried	1 cup	4 ounces	120 grams
Fruits or veggies, chopped	1 cup	5 to 7 ounces	145 to 200 grams
Fruits or veggies, puréed	1 cup	8.5 ounces	245 grams
Honey, maple syrup, or corn syrup	1 tablespoon	.75 ounce	20 grams
Liquids: cream, milk, water, or juice	1 cup	8 fluid ounces	240 milliliters
Oats	1 cup	5.5 ounces	150 grams
Salt	1 teaspoon	0.2 ounce	6 grams
Spices: cinnamon, cloves, ginger, or nutmeg (ground)	1 teaspoon	0.2 ounce	5 milliliters
Sugar, brown, firmly packed	1 cup	7 ounces	200 grams
Sugar, white	1 cup/1 tablespoon	7 ounces/0.5 ounce	200 grams/12.5 grams
Vanilla extract	1 teaspoon	0.2 ounce	4 grams

Fahrenheit	Celsius	Gas Mark
225°	110°	1/4
250°	120°	1/2
275°	140°	1
300°	150°	2
325°	160°	3
350°	180°	4
375°	190°	5
400°	200°	6
425°	220°	7
450°	230°	8

Editorial Note: Original measurements from the first German edition appear in parentheses for all recipes. We strongly suggest readers use these measurements throughout, but we have converted many for use by home cooks who do not have access to electronic scales in their kitchens.

Originally published by 2015 Verlag Georg D.W. Callwey GmbH & Co. KG, Munchen, Germany in 2015.

English manuscript © 2015 by Cathleen Clarity

First Skyhorse Publishing edition, 2017

Skyhorse Publishing books may be purchased in bulk at special discounts for sales promotion, corporate gifts, fund-raising, or educational purposes. Special editions can also be created to specifications. For details, contact the Special Sales Department, Skyhorse Publishing, 307 West 36th Street, 11th Floor, New York, NY 10018 or info@skyhorsepublishing.com.

Skyhorse® and Skyhorse Publishing® are registered trademarks of Skyhorse Publishing, Inc.®, a Delaware corporation.

Visit our website at www.skyhorsepublishing.com.

10 9 8 7 6 5 4 3 2 1

Library of Congress Cataloging-in-Publication Data is available on file.

Cover design by Amanda Jane Jones
Cover photo credit: Kathrin Koschitzki

Print ISBN: 978-1-5107-2113-5
Ebook ISBN: 978-1-5107-2117-3

Printed in China